GRACE MOMENTS
OCTOBER–DECEMBER 2025

Published by Straight Talk Books
P.O. Box 301, Milwaukee, WI 53201
800.661.3311 / timeofgrace.org

Copyright © 2025 Time of Grace Ministry

All rights reserved. This publication may not be copied, photocopied, reproduced, translated, or converted to any electronic or machine-readable form in whole or in part, except for brief quotations, without prior written approval from Time of Grace Ministry.

Unless otherwise indicated, Scripture is taken from THE HOLY BIBLE, NEW INTERNATIONAL VERSION®, NIV® Copyright © 1973, 1978, 1984, 2011 by Biblica, Inc.® Used by permission. All rights reserved worldwide.

Scripture quotations marked ESV are taken from The Holy Bible, English Standard Version®. Text Edition: 2016. Copyright © 2001 by Crossway, a publishing ministry of Good News Publishers. All rights reserved.

Scripture quotations marked GW are taken from GOD'S WORD®. © 1995, 2003, 2013, 2014, 2019, 2020 by God's Word to the Nations Mission Society. Used by permission.

Printed in the United States of America
ISBN: 978-1-965694-30-5

TIME OF GRACE *is a registered mark of Time of Grace Ministry.*

OCTOBER

"Give, and it will be given to you.
A good measure, pressed down, shaken together
and running over, will be poured into your lap.
For with the measure you use,
it will be measured to you."

LUKE 6:38

October 1

Generous people change people's lives
Mike Novotny

When Kim and I got married, we were 22 and really broke. She was a kindergarten teacher in a Christian school (a.k.a. not a millionaire), and I was working a smattering of part-time jobs cutting grass, driving a Zamboni, and tutoring in Spanish (a.k.a. also not a millionaire). But Kim's parents, truly generous people, changed our lives with their generosity. They gave us a wedding gift that helped us take those first steps in our new life together. To this day, I am so grateful for their open hearts and open hands.

In our ad-filled world, we are inundated with messages about getting. "Get _____, and you'll be happier/cooler/prettier/more popular/finally content!" But Jesus would tell you today what he told his followers back in the day: **"It is more blessed to give than to receive"** (Acts 20:35). Giving not only blesses the recipient but also blesses the giver.

God would tell you that there is a sweet happiness that givers experience. The Father who gave his one and only Son, the Son who gave his one and only life, and the Spirit who gives life through the gift of faith are the happiest trio you will ever meet. They are eternal examples of the blessedness of generosity. I pray that we all can walk in their footsteps today.

Is there a specific way that you could experience that blessing today?

October 2

My big God
Liz Schroeder

Indulge me for a moment as I tell you about my husband, John—affectionately known around here as My Big Man. At 6'4", he is almost a full ruler taller than I am. He's easy to spot in a crowd, and when we go shopping, I never stress about reaching anything on the top shelf. But my favorite part? When he hugs me, my head rests right over his heart.

Now imagine me trying to carry John in my jeans pocket. Absurd, right? If it's silly to think I could fit a grown man in my pocket, how much more ridiculous is it to try and fit GOD into my limited expectations?

Yet, when I start editing what I'll accept as answers to my prayers, that's exactly what I do. I treat the Creator of the universe like my divine personal assistant. In the immortal words of the genie from *Aladdin*: "Phenomenal cosmic powers! Itty-bitty living space."

But then God reminds me in Isaiah 55:9: **"As the heavens are higher than the earth, so are my ways higher than your ways and my thoughts than your thoughts."**

Forget using a ruler; My Big God's thoughts and plans are higher than mine by light-years. Maybe that means I can trust him with what I don't yet understand. Maybe I don't need all the answers to walk in faith today.

And maybe—just maybe—I can rest my head over his heart, like I do with John, trusting My Big God to hold me.

October 3

An unlikely favorite Bible promise
Dave Burleton

What's your all-time favorite promise from God in the Bible? Perhaps it's this: **"Never will I leave you; never will I forsake you"** (Hebrews 13:5). Or, **"Surely I am with you always, to the very end of the age"** (Matthew 28:20).

I have a very nontraditional answer to my all-time favorite promise of God. It's John 16:33. What's promised at the beginning of that verse? **"In this world you will have trouble."**

I told you it was an unlikely choice! So why does this promise mean so much to me? Pastor Mike Novotny once shared a simple formula for joy: *Joy = Results - Expectations*. This promise from God clearly sets the appropriate expectations for our lives as Christians in this fallen world so we can find true joy during our time here on the earth.

Should we have an expectation that through faith we will have problem-free lives that are the envy of our neighborhoods? Not according to John 16:33. So when problems arise (and they will), I pray remembering this promise will help you not feel your faith being shaken or your joy being robbed. And then, you and I can dwell on the second promise found in that very same verse: **"But take heart! I have overcome the world."** We need not fear or be discouraged by any problem this world throws at us because Jesus our Savior has overcome this world and earned for us a perfect forever home in heaven.

October 4

Zing!
Clark Schultz

Have you ever been zinged? You're belting out the lyrics to your favorite song. A friend or spouse asks you innocently, "Who sings that song?"

You go from soloist to proud band supporter, saying, "Why, it's U2!"

And the friend/spouse replies, "Then let's just let them sing it."

ZING!

King David was singing another tune. His chorus started with boredom; this led to the second verse of adultery, followed by a pregnancy with another man's wife. David's refrain sang of a cover-up that led to a final verse of murder.

Enter Nathan, the prophet of God who shared with David a touching story of a lamb that was stolen and killed by a rich neighbor. David's anger burned against this selfish man. With the ultimate zinger, Nathan replied to David, **"You are the man!"** (2 Samuel 12:7). ZING!

What song or sin are you singing? Is it a new tune, or is it the same-old harmony and pet sin you know too well? Take a page or note from King David and pray, sing, or shout off-key Psalm 51: **"Have mercy on me, O God, according to your unfailing love; according to your great compassion blot out my transgressions. Wash away all my iniquity and cleanse me from my sin"** (verses 1,2).

Perhaps it's this devotion or a friend who needs to zing you. Instead of a cover-up, go to the One who covers over all your sins with the blood of his Son. That's a song you and I never grow tired of singing.

October 5

No matter how small
Liz Schroeder

Dr. Seuss got it right in *Horton Hears a Who!* He said that no matter how small a person is, they are still a person. Horton, an elephant with a heart of gold, risks everything to protect a tiny world living on a speck of dust. Why? Because he knows the people matter—even if they're microscopic. That's not just good storytelling; it's a surprisingly accurate glimpse into the heart of God.

"Though the Lord is exalted, he looks kindly on the lowly; though lofty, he sees them from afar" (Psalm 138:6).

God doesn't wait for us to grow up, glow up, or get it together. He's not withholding love until we earn a spiritual gold star. He meets us right where we are: anxious, unqualified, and likely running late. Again.

Grace isn't a paycheck for good behavior; it's a gift from the Giver.

While the world gives the mic to the loudest voice in the room, God leans in to hear the quiet ones: the overlooked, the overworked, those muttering, "Lord, help." You are not invisible. You are handpicked, pursued, and cherished by the God who designed galaxies . . . and still notices when you're on your last nerve.

Once you believe that, even the boring stuff gets anointed with meaning. That daily commute? A one-to-one talk with the Almighty. Those tricky emails? A chance to reflect Jesus with gentleness. Even that dreaded meeting becomes an honors course in advanced discipleship.

So stand tall, especially when you feel small. God sees you and hears you, because in his kingdom, the hurting and humble always have his ear.

October 6

The biggest danger of wanting more money
Mike Novotny

In 2021 a herd of 15 elephants escaped a Chinese nature preserve and wandered the countryside. No one knew where the alpha male was taking them, but they were farther and farther from where they started.

That picture made me think of Paul's warning: **"Some people, eager for money, have wandered from the faith"** (1 Timothy 6:10). Eager for extra dollars, some people wandered. They didn't reject or renounce Jesus. They just wandered from him.

A danger we all face—especially during our post-high school days as we establish our careers—is to wander unintentionally from the faith by losing our connection to the Word that gives faith (Romans 10:17). Lose your Sunday church habit and your daily devotion, and you will not have the kind of strong and growing faith that your Father wants you to have. You may still pray and you may not end up as an atheist, but your faith will not be charged up by the power cord of God's Word.

So if you have to choose, be strong and courageous, and don't wander from God's Word. Ask your manager about options, and don't be ashamed to tell them about your love for Jesus. He is your greatest treasure and the One you seek before all else.

God wants to keep you close. That's why he sent his Son to draw you near to his presence. That's why he gave his Spirit to work faith in your heart. That's why he gave his Word so you could read, listen, and meditate on the love that is yours in Jesus.

October 7

A high standard of love
Andrea Delwiche

Psalm 144 is traditionally thought of as David's prayer for deliverance for Israel: **"Rescue me and deliver me from the hand of foreigners, whose mouths speak lies and whose right hand is a right hand of falsehood. May our cattle be heavy with young, suffering no mishap or failure in bearing; may there be no cry of distress in our streets! Blessed are the people to whom such blessings fall! Blessed are the people whose God is the Lord!"** (verses 11,14,15 ESV). This psalm appeals to our own longings for our world to feel safe. Security is a gift of God, as evidenced by David's own prayer.

Sometimes our desire for security leads us to react in fear toward others. We selfishly desire to change people and situations to fit our own mold. We make excuses to violate God's command to love God and neighbors as we love ourselves.

God's people are to show love and welcome people who bring nothing to the table except their own neediness—the state of all of us before God and each other. God defined himself to Moses: **"The Lord, a God merciful and gracious, slow to anger, and abounding in steadfast love and faithfulness, keeping steadfast love for thousands, forgiving iniquity and transgression and sin, but who will by no means clear the guilty"** (Exodus 34:6,7 ESV).

God's character is further revealed to us in Jesus, who famously said, **"Let the little children come"** (Matthew 19:14 ESV) and held his church to the highest standard of love and mercy.

October 8

Defining freedom
Dave Burleton

I'd venture to claim that "freedom" is an idea with a nearly universal approval rating amongst constituents from all walks of life. What politician or party in our country doesn't espouse freedom as a core principle for what they fight for? It's when you attempt to define that word, though, that you start to see the fractures of differing opinions and viewpoints that can lead to a country with some significant political polarization. So what does freedom mean to you? Or perhaps the real question to ask is: What does freedom mean to you as a Christian, bought and redeemed by the blood of Christ on Calvary?

I'm rather fond of one definition that is attributed to Abraham Lincoln: "Freedom is not the right to do what we want, but what we ought." Jesus did not die on a cross to give you and me license to sin in perpetuity, safe in the knowledge of our Redeemer. Instead, that redemption story stirs our hearts to strive to be disciples of Jesus, turning from our selfish ways and taking up our crosses to follow him. As Peter shared in his epistle, **"Live as people who are free, not using your freedom as a cover-up for evil, but living as servants of God"** (2 Peter 2:16 ESV).

Give praise for the freedom that Christ's victory won for you, and honor his priceless gift by exercising the freedom to do what you ought to his glory. Love like Jesus. Serve like your Lord. Share grace like your Redeemer.

October 9

Open kimono
Liz Schroeder

I can't imagine my life without a life group. Whether you call it a life group, small group, growth group, or community group, the goal is the same: gather around God's Word and pray for one another during the week.

After a year of meeting together, our group wanted to go deeper. To give context to our prayer requests and deepen our relationships, we decided to share our life stories. Each person told their full story, including the hard parts, with an emphasis on where they saw God at work.

Before my husband's turn, I asked how vulnerable he planned to be. He simply said, "I'm going 'open kimono'." It doesn't get more transparent than that.

But that kind of openness only happens when trust is strong. From the beginning, we committed to confidentiality. Knowing that what's shared in the group stays in the group has given us the freedom to be real. Without that sacred trust, vulnerability wouldn't be possible.

The results have been rich and healing. We've laughed at shared memories, found common ground, and made sure no one cried alone. Most important, we've practiced confession and forgiveness. It's become a space where we're fully known and deeply loved.

James affirms this: **"Therefore confess your sins to each other and pray for each other so that you may be healed"** (James 5:16).

What if someone needs to hear your "open kimono" story? Vulnerability, rooted in Christ, may be the very thing that brings hope to someone else.

October 10

As precious as silver and gold
Dave Burleton

Perhaps, like me, you had a stage in your teenage years when you fancied yourself a star-crossed poet. In those handwritten notes and letters to the object of your affection, you toiled over just the right metaphor to describe how precious, how valuable, how beautiful that person was in your eyes. Did you know that God has some very flattering metaphors for describing how he feels about you?

Proverbs 17:3 compares your heart to precious metals like gold and silver. Your heart, your soul—YOU are truly precious to him. But the metaphor goes even further as the Lord reminds you how silver and gold reach their full beauty and strength: **"The crucible for silver, and the furnace for gold."** And in that same spirit, **"The Lord tests the heart."**

How's that for reframing your mindset? The Lord tests your heart because you are as precious and valuable to him as silver and gold! The hardships of life occur because the Lord sees your full value as his own child, to further refine you as a true disciple of Jesus.

So today, if you find yourself questioning your worth, think of this verse in Proverbs and tell yourself that you are precious to God. That's the very reason why you and I can **"glory in our sufferings"** (Romans 5:3)!

October 11

Not forgotten
Clark Schultz

Mary Helen Hoff, the wife of a U.S. military officer listed as missing in action during the Vietnam War, developed the idea for a national flag to remind every American of the U.S. service members whose fates were never accounted for during the war. The POW/MIA flag with a black-and-white image of a gaunt silhouette, a strand of barbed wire, and an ominous watchtower was designed by Newt Heisley, a former World War II pilot.

With all due respect to those who served, are serving, or have lost or never had closure with their loved ones, my heart goes out to you. No one can ever know what you are feeling, and my prayers are with you.

Spiritually speaking, you and I are prisoners of war too. Prisoners to sins of habit, greed, and selfishness. We are constantly at war against temptations. Jesus entered a synagogue in Luke 4:18 and into our sin-captive hearts with words from the prophet Isaiah: **"The Spirit of the Lord is on me. . . . He has sent me to proclaim freedom for the prisoners . . . to set the oppressed free."** Talk about a mind bend. Jesus read words that were written about 700 years earlier about himself! Jesus is the only one who sets us free from sin. The Spirit opens our eyes to the truth of being saved by God's grace alone. Jesus, "the Anointed One," took the punishment we deserved and set us free.

Just like the POW/MIA flag states, we too are not forgotten but are 100% forgiven.

October 12

A change in the weather
Daron Lindemann

A foggy, autumn haze shrouded my front yard. It filtered the early morning sunrise through gray tones of orange. An hour later, a beautiful, clear day of sunshine arrived. The vibrant colors of the landscape, the green grass and leaves on the trees turning reddish yellow, changed my front yard. Dramatically.

It made me think of these words of God: **"I have swept away your offenses like a cloud, your sins like the morning mist. Return to me, for I have redeemed you"** (Isaiah 44:22).

A change in the weather can really change your outlook, right? Well, if that's what God (not Mother Nature) can do for you with the weather . . . Think of the billions of tiny vapor droplets in a cloud of morning mist, and God sweeps them away with a little sunshine and breeze. Now think of the numerous mistakes you've made, promises you've broken, and words you've regretted. God sweeps them away "like the morning mist."

God clears up your life, your conscience, and your view of today's circumstances for you to see your Redeemer, Jesus. You are free and clear to return to him without a cloud of sin or shame hanging over you. He's not offended. You are forgiven.

The vibrant beauty of God's redeeming grace gives you clarity that is clearer than a bright, sunny fall day full of color. Brighten your day with clear faith in his vibrant promises.

October 13

Revived by grace
Liz Schroeder

Naomi detoxed during ten days in jail, but 72 hours after her release, she overdosed on fentanyl and died. Four doses of Narcan* jolted her body back to life. The next day she celebrated her first sober birthday in a decade.

Today, Naomi's face glows with health and hope. At her rock bottom, she encountered God's presence and power. She's hungry for more, convinced God has a plan for her life, and eager to discover what it is.

Her story might sound extraordinary, but the pattern isn't. It's the spiritual journey of every believer. In Ephesians 2, Paul explains: **"You were dead in your transgressions and sins. But because of his great love for us, God, who is rich in mercy, made us alive with Christ even when we were dead in transgressions—it is by grace you have been saved"** (verses 1,4,5).

We were all dead. Just as opioids suppress breathing, sin smothers the soul. Just as Naomi couldn't revive herself, neither could we. Only the Holy Spirit can breathe life into what was lifeless.

Take a moment and ask the Lord, "Now what?" Read the whole chapter of Ephesians 2. Camp out on verse 10: **"We are God's handiwork, created in Christ Jesus to do good works, which God prepared in advance for us to do."** And please join me in a prayer of thanks for all the Naomis out there.

---

* Narcan (naloxone) works by blocking the effects of opioids. It is a life-saving tool widely carried by EMTs and rehab staff, but everyday heroes carry it to help save the lives of people affected by opioid misuse.

October 14

It all changed
Jon Enter

If you could pick any ferocious, wild animal to be your pet, which animal would you choose? Wild animals can be tamed, but they're also documented to return to their animal instincts to attack or kill their owners. That's scary.

Did you know that prior to the flood, animals didn't fear humans? When Noah stepped off the ark on Mount Ararat, God said this: **"The fear and dread of you will fall on all the beasts . . . birds . . . on every creature that moves along the ground . . . and on all the fish. . . . Everything that lives and moves about will be food for you"** (Genesis 9:2,3). Prior to the flood, Noah and his family quite possibly could've had lions, tigers, and bears as pets. Oh my! After the flood, Noah and his family would've been the first humans to ever enjoy a steak dinner.

After the flood, life forever changed! Our lifespans changed and shortened. Our diets changed and included meat. Our need for an umbrella changed as now it regularly rains (Genesis 2:6).

God, however, is unchanging. The same loving Lord who preserved Noah's family through the flood is watching over you. The same loving Lord who blessed Noah's family as they restarted in life is with you. You have nothing to fear.

Storms will come. With Jesus in your heart, you will rise above. It doesn't mean it won't be difficult. Life is. **"But those who hope in the Lord will renew their strength"** (Isaiah 40:31). He keeps his promises. Always.

October 15

Saints on screens
Mike Novotny

When I consider my own relationship with screens, which has been a roller coaster of joy and regret, I find myself turning back to the wisdom of Jesus:

"A certain man was preparing a great banquet and invited many guests. At the time of the banquet he sent his servant to tell those who had been invited, 'Come, for everything is now ready.' But they all alike began to make excuses. The first said, 'I have just bought a field, and I must go and see it. Please excuse me.' Another said, 'I have just bought five yoke of oxen, and I'm on my way to try them out. Please excuse me.' Still another said, 'I just got married, so I can't come'" (Luke 14:16-20).

Notice three things about this brilliantly crafted story. First, a generous man gives a free invitation to a "great banquet," a rare treat in a time and place where most people didn't eat meat. Second, notice how everyone excuses themselves to do things that are not necessarily bad. Finally, notice the inaccurate way they decline the invitation: Must? Can't? Would you die if you came to the banquet and then went home to your field or your wife?

Take a moment to apply those three points to your relationship with screens. While hours of streaming shows and social media might not be wrong, are they getting in the way of a greater feast that Jesus is inviting you to enjoy?

October 16

Let's not "rage quit"
Clark Schultz

My middle son dropped a phrase I've never heard before: *rage quit*. After watching our team give up two touchdowns at the start of the fourth quarter, we shut the TV off. My wife asked how the game ended. Son 2 quickly said, "We stunk, so we rage quitted," which means "to abandon an activity or pursuit that has become frustrating, especially the playing of a video game."

One can beg to differ that this phrase has to do with just video games. Sticking to the diet? Drinking less caffeine? Limiting your screen time? Setting more time aside for prayer? In the game of life, the good things we should be doing—portion control, more water, and a ton of Jesus—often become the first things we "rage quit" on. Perhaps it's because God's timetable and ours don't line up. Struggles, setbacks, and sins frustrate our efforts too.

Paul wrote, **"Therefore, my dear brothers and sisters, stand firm. Let nothing move you"** (1 Corinthians 15:58). How do we not rage quit on the good and godly things such as spending regular time in God's Word, building others up instead of tearing them down, or showing humility instead of pride? 1) Look to the One who has and will never rage quit on you. God sent Jesus so you will never be alone. He will give you strength to keep going. 2) Look for friends, family, and a church family to encourage you.

October 17

Firstfruits of your time
Dave Burleton

Do you recall the Genesis account of Cain and Abel when God accepted Abel's sacrifice while rejecting Cain's offering? Through this account, we learn that God truly desires thank offerings that are given with a heart that is compelled to share our best with him, our firstfruits.

Perhaps it's stories from the Bible like this or simply the strong visual image that a term like *firstfruits* evokes for me, but I find it so easy to focus simply on tangible gifts that I give to the Lord and for his kingdom. However, as a student of Aristotle named Theophrastus once wrote, "Time is the most valuable thing that a man can spend."

What could giving our Savior the firstfruits of our time look like? We would have prayer and time spent in his Word scheduled into our daily calendars in ink. Going further, we could schedule it at the time of day when we are at our peak ability to focus (the early morning for me, personally), not at the end of an exhausting day that leaves us wanting to just reach for our TV remotes or our pillows.

And when we do so, God has promised to bless us beyond measure: **"Honor the Lord with your wealth, with the firstfruits of all your crops; then your barns will be filled to overflowing, and your vats will brim over with new wine"** (Proverbs 3:9,10). Let's commit to giving our Lord the very best of our most valuable earthly resource, our time, and see how he blesses us throughout each day!

October 18

Surprise party
Liz Schroeder

One week before his 40th birthday surprise party, Kenny surprised us all by passing away peacefully on his living room couch. No one saw it coming.

Ken was an artist. The day after he died, his beloved Linda gave me the piece he had been working on for my birthday. Using pencil and ink, Ken drew a victorious Jesus, complete with sword and halo. He sketched a dove above Jesus' left shoulder, and Kenny creatively incorporated my name and the name of our church. But what really stands out is the smile on Jesus' face. It shines more than the halo.

Kenny drew a joyful Jesus because he knew a joyful Jesus. As a recovering addict, Ken could've gotten stuck in shame, weighed down by his sin. He knew well what God demands, because our recovery meetings focus the first half of every lesson on the law and how we've fallen short. But the meetings don't end there. The second half turns our eyes to the cross, where grace speaks louder than guilt.

Kenny didn't earn his way into heaven. He was carried there by mercy. Jesus saw Kenny coming and welcomed his weary brother home—with outstretched arms and a smile on his face.

"The Lord is close to the brokenhearted and saves those who are crushed in spirit" (Psalm 34:18).

We miss Kenny, but he didn't miss the party. Jesus had a celebration waiting for him. **"There is rejoicing in the presence of the angels of God over one sinner who repents"** (Luke 15:10).

October 19

Grace through the storm
Jon Enter

During Noah's life, the human race was only evil all the time (Genesis 6:5). That's why God sent the floodwaters to destroy the earth. Even in this judgment, God showed mercy.

Noah built an ark. That took a long time—time for the people to repent. Noah grew, harvested, and stored all the food for all the animals. That took time—time for the people to repent. God said to Noah's family, **"Go into the ark. . . . Seven days from now I will send rain on the earth"** (Genesis 7:1,4). The people saw animals parade into the ark two by two, and they should've realized God was serious. They got another seven days to repent. They didn't. The rain started.

Bible scholars believe it hadn't rained before the flood. Dews watered the earth (Genesis 2:6). When the flood started, the water canopy and water storehouse (Genesis 1:6-8) both burst (Genesis 7:11). When rain fell, **"the Lord shut** [Noah's family] **in,"** sealing them in grace (Genesis 7:16).

God showed grace before, during, and after the flood. He sustained life on that smelly, floating zoo for a year. God then promised through a rainbow never to destroy all life in a flood again. A rainbow happened. It rained! That must've been terrifying! But Noah saw God's mercy.

What's scaring you? Look through what's scary, and see God guiding you. He surrounds you with his grace during and after the storms of life. He simply asks for your trust.

October 20

I need you, Lord
Andrea Delwiche

"I call to you, Lord, come quickly to me; hear me when I call to you. May my prayer be set before you like incense; may the lifting up of my hands be like the evening sacrifice" (Psalm 141:1,2).

Sometimes we don't have a lot of energy or joy for anything, even for God. Life's problems loom large, sucking our energy, distracting us from good intentions. We grab onto anything we find to distract us. God's calling to us, but we aren't sure we have the desire to listen.

Maybe we are so overwhelmed that we are finally in a place of humility before God. Even though we acknowledge our place as people who need help, we cannot articulate it.

It seems in this psalm that David is too tired, frightened, angry to do anything "religious." But he knows he needs God's presence to sustain him. It's as if he's saying: "I need you right now, Lord. All I can do is beg for your help. I lay my need, humility, and love for you on the altar. Let my weakness and desire for you be more tangible and acceptable than the traces of smoke and incense rising to heaven."

This is a transparent plea. God's promise is equally transparent and reliable. Our plea *is* acceptable to God. God reassures us over and over in the pages of Scripture: When we seek him, we will find him, for he has already found us. Like lambs on the Shepherd's shoulders, we are held securely by his love.

October 21

One more day
Jon Enter

You can endure almost anything if you know it will end. Mothers who give birth talk about this. The pain of childbirth is excruciating but temporary, and the reward of holding your newborn makes it worthwhile. Marathon runners endure the pain of each pounding stride, counting down until the 26.2-mile finish line.

What life pain are you enduring? What has you exhausted and overwhelmed so you don't know if you can hold on much longer?

Throughout the Bible, God's people endured unimaginable pains. It rained 40 days for the flood. Noah wondered if it would ever stop. The Israelites wandered in the wilderness 40 years. They wondered if their wandering would ever cease. Goliath taunted the Israelites 40 days. They wondered who could ever defeat him.

Each of these 40 days/years of pain ended with a 41. On day 41, the rain stopped. On year 41, the wandering stopped. On day 41, Goliath was dead.

I have a new favorite number: 41. Each time frame of 40 in the Bible that has suffering, waiting, and wondering ends with 41. It ends. God triumphs. God releases. God restores. God provides.

What pain are you enduring? What has you exhausted or overwhelmed? You are in your time of waiting, but you don't wait alone. God is with you, sustaining you, strengthening you, giving you all you need to endure. Hold on. **"Wait for the Lord; be strong and take heart and wait for the Lord"** (Psalm 27:14). Your 41 is coming.

October 22

The desperate love of God
Mike Novotny

At the end of one of Jesus' parables, we get a stunning look at God's heart. The story begins with a generous master inviting people to a "great banquet," which, sadly, everyone is too busy to attend.

"The servant came back and reported this to his master. Then the owner of the house became angry and ordered his servant, 'Go out quickly into the streets and alleys of the town and bring in the poor, the crippled, the blind and the lame.' 'Sir,' the servant said, 'what you ordered has been done, but there is still room.' Then the master told his servant, 'Go out to the roads and country lanes and compel them to come in, so that my house will be full. I tell you, not one of those who were invited will get a taste of my banquet'" (Luke 14:21-24).

Those final words are a warning about rejecting Jesus' generous invitation. But notice what precedes them—a master who is passionate, perhaps even desperate, to fill his house with guests. "Go out!" he commands his servant on two separate occasions to search the streets, alleys, roads, and lanes to bring in the poor, crippled, blind, and lame. No matter who they are, the master wants them to feast by his side.

This is Jesus' way of saying that God wants you. You might feel poor, spiritually crippled, unworthy to be with God, but that's not true. God wants his house full. He wants you to sit by him at the great feast of heaven.

What an invitation! What a God!

October 23

When evil surrounds you
Jon Enter

Life's hard. You're bombarded by endless decisions. Those decisions have consequences. Life's made more difficult when the consequences of other people's decisions hurt you.

That was the life of Noah. God described the moral compass of Noah's neighbors in this eye-opening way. **"Every inclination of the thoughts of the human heart was only evil all the time"** (Genesis 6:5). Something had to be done to bring balance to the earth. Something big.

God hit the reset button on the human race by preserving the one family that still honored him. **"Noah was a righteous man, blameless among the people of his time"** (Genesis 6:9). Notice it doesn't say Noah was perfect. But he worked hard to do what was right even when others did wrong.

That's a hard road to walk. It's extremely difficult to stand firm on righteousness when others don't or won't. Because when they notice you, you become the target of their evil.

It's always right to do what's right even if that brings judgment. God is powerful. God is protective of his people. God's miraculous rescue of Noah through the global floodwaters on a wooden ark brings hope that God sees your suffering and acts. Far greater than the rescue of Noah was God's rescue of the world through a wooden cross. He saw the world's suffering, and he acted.

Are you weary in enduring what's right? Read God's rescue plan of Noah in Genesis 6–9, and know the Lord cherishes you just as much as Noah.

October 24

Always a win-win situation
Clark Schultz

While driving my minivan, I like to point out to my children each car on the highway as a Ford, Dodge, or Chevy. Each manufacturer makes their own version of what my boys call "a cool car." One day, a lime-green Ford Mustang GT passed us by, and our middle son said, "Dad, that must be a plumber who owns that. Plumbers are super rich."

Are you rich? Blessed? The devil is slick at making us think that if we don't have the latest and the greatest tech, clothes, and automobiles, we must be poor. A family friend used to say this phrase: "I wonder what the rich people are doing." He usually said it to family and friends he hadn't seen in a while when the sun was shining over a grilled hamburger and a cold beverage. His thought was that richness can often be found in the simple things of life.

For the apostle Paul, life was a win-win situation of being rich and blessed by living each day for Jesus. He said, **"For to me, to live is Christ and to die is gain"** (Philippians 1:21). The life Paul lived with suffering and loss was focused on Christ and letting others see Christ as more than cool but as their Savior. The flip side was that if God were to call him home, he would be eternally rich and blessed in the presence of Jesus by grace.

Plumber, minivan, or Mustang, you are always in a win-win situation with Jesus.

October 25

You are not them
Mike Novotny

People are not equal. You might think that statement is insultingly obvious, but I find it hard to remember. What I find very easy to believe, however, is that I should be equal to them.

When I was a brand-new pastor, I listened to the podcasts of one of America's most popular preachers. This guy was bold, passionate, intuitive, and so many other amazing things that I wasn't. One night I was listening to one of his sermons, overwhelmed by his gifts, and I felt worthless. I walked out of my house, wandered over to a park, sat on a bench, and broke down. I begged God to help me be better, different. Because in that moment, I believed that people should be equal.

Do you too? He can talk to anyone without social anxiety—you should be that confident. She tells everyone about Jesus so naturally—why can't you evangelize like that? He has so many great ideas—why can't you think of one good one? She prays without preparing—you stutter and can't think of anything to say. So often when you feel jealous or useless, it's because you believe that people should be equal.

Meditate on the following truth until it frees you from this soul-sapping lie: **"Each of you should use whatever gift you have received to serve others"** (1 Peter 4:10). God may have given you the same saving grace as others, but your gift is yours and their gift is theirs. Confusing the two will crush you.

Be you today, because God didn't make people equal.

October 26

They are not you
Mike Novotny

People are not equal. You might think that statement is insultingly obvious, but I find it absurdly hard to remember. What I find very easy to believe, however, is that they should be just like me. Do you believe that too?

Why can't my classmates just care about this group project (like I do) and work ahead on their part (like I did) and believe that GPA really, really matters (like I do)? Why can't my boyfriend just organize his life (like I do), write things down in a calendar (like I do), and stick to the original plan (like I do)? Why is she so grumpy when plans change (I'm not)? Why does he fill every second of silence with words (I don't)? Why don't they just say something (I am)? It's so frustrating when people aren't just like you or me.

I bet you need Paul's words as much as I do today: **"But in fact God has placed the parts in the body, every one of them, just as he wanted them to be"** (1 Corinthians 12:18). We have much in common: the same sinfulness, the same Savior, the same God and Father. But you and I and he and she and they are vastly different parts in this "body" we call God's family.

Let them be them today, because God didn't make people equal.

October 27

Sandcastle or surfboard?
Dave Burleton

If you're like me, a family vacation to the beach isn't complete without taking a moment or two simply to sit back and marvel at the power and relentlessness of ocean waves. Are they beautiful or terrifying? Yes! Are they constructive sources of energy or destructive forces of chaos? Again, yes! It's a matter of perspective. It depends if you are a sandcastle or a surfboard.

Think about our lives and the role that unexpected change plays into our time here on the earth. Change is powerful, disruptive, and will never stop coming, just like the waves of the ocean. So if we can't stop change from happening to us, how can we position ourselves to thrive within it? We need to be surfboards, not sandcastles.

Let's start by realizing that as powerful as those ocean waves are or the change in our lives feels, the Creator of all things is infinitely more powerful. In Isaiah 43:1 our Lord assures us, **"Do not fear, for I have redeemed you; I have summoned you by name; you are mine."** We can work confidently to flourish in our faith journeys through change because we are his, called by name and dearly beloved. So ride atop those waves of change, and let them bring you closer to Jesus because **"in all your ways submit to him, and he will make your paths straight"** (Proverbs 3:6).

October 28

Your Father
Clark Schultz

It's an often-quoted movie line. In the culmination scene of the movie *The Empire Strikes Back*,* the antagonist, Darth Vader, asks the protagonist, Luke Skywalker, to join him on the dark side. Luke says, "You killed my father." Vader replies, "No, I am your father." Cue Father of the Year award here.

Abraham from the Bible was father to the nation of Israel. Yet "father" Abraham might not win any Father of the Year awards either. He lied about his wife being his sister *twice*. He tried to speed up God's plan of the Savior by sleeping with his wife's maidservant.

What makes Abraham important is *his* heavenly Father—*El-Shaddai*: **"I am God Almighty"** (Genesis 17:1). God Almighty gave a seasoned Abraham a son who would carry the line of the Savior. The same Almighty made it possible for Mary the mother of the promised Savior to sing: **"For the Mighty One has done great things for me"** (Luke 1:49).

He is the same Father and El Shaddai whom we have today. Do you and I deserve him? No, we too make lying our native language and try to tell God how to do his job. But none of that takes away from the love of the Father in his Son, Jesus.

Fathers aren't perfect, but my prayer is that the next generation knows the truth that sets them free: *God* is our Father.

---

* Folks, the movie is 45 years old, so apologies if I'm spoiling this for you.

October 29

Heliocentric in prayer
Dave Burleton

In 1543 the astronomer Copernicus set off a powder keg of controversy when he published a paper stating the case for heliocentricity in our solar system. Simply put, he used mathematics to demonstrate that the stars and planets seen in the night sky don't revolve around Earth but instead around the sun. He said humankind's home is not the center of the universe. Instead an amazingly powerful source of life-giving energy is truly at the center.

What does this have to do with prayer life? I'd encourage you to do an audit of your last prayer session with God. What topic did you lead off with? What issues did you spend the most time focusing on? If you and I are honest, we may have been placing ourselves at the center and trying to persuade or compel God to provide what we were asking for. We may have ended our prayer with, "Your will be done," when our hearts were really feeling, "May your will be what I want to be done."

So how could a sun-centered model help realign your prayer life? Your heart orbits around your Creator and Redeemer, wholly dependent on him. Focus on his kingdom and serve him by showing love, grace, and truth to those around you. Ask God for help to accept, understand, and be grateful for his infinitely wise plan for your life. After all, God **"is able to do immeasurably more than all we ask or imagine, according to his power that is at work within us"** (Ephesians 3:20).

October 30

Level ground
Andrea Delwiche

If you've ever been hiking, you know what it's like to hope for a level path. After a tough vertical ascent, a level path is a gift, a chance to swallow some water, marvel over where you've been, and anticipate where you're going. But all this requires submitting to the path, following its curves and climbs, trusting that it will lead you to your destination.

Often my trust in God is hedged by my own desires, and it's hard for me to pray, "Your will be done." Sometimes I have a skewed picture of God as an angry God who doesn't love me unconditionally. When this picture of God rears its ugly head, I struggle to trust him to lead me.

Perhaps that's why these words from Psalm 143 relieve some of my anxiety: **"Teach me to do your will, for you are my God; may your good Spirit lead me on level ground"** (verse 10). This is the same God of whom the apostle John says, **"God is light; in him there is no darkness at all"** (1 John 1:5). Jesus' brother James reminds us that God **"does not change like shifting shadows"** (James 1:17).

God is good. He sees and loves me. I can look forward to following God's path, led by his understanding of what I need.

Your path through life is tiring. You may wonder if you can make it. But God is working to bring you to the level place. His good Spirit loves and leads you. As you need it, he stretches out his arms—and carries you.

October 31

Mr. Beast and our Messiah
Mike Novotny

Have you heard of *Beast Games*, the insane reality show run by YouTube star Mr. Beast? In one scene, Mr. Beast asks four teams to pick a captain. The twist: Mr. Beast bribes those captains to sell out their teammates for stacks of cash.

The four captains climb up a tower to Mr. Beast. There's a giant button in front of them and a scoreboard behind them counting up with the bribe. Would they send their teammates home for $10,000? $50,000? How about $100,000? $500,000? $1,000,000?!

Here's the beast you have to wrestle with in real life: You can't have both the riches of this world and the spiritual riches of Jesus. You can't do what you want, believe what you want, and behave how you want and expect to be an accepted member of Team Jesus. Sadly, people trade fellowship with Jesus for some lesser thing every day. They follow their hearts, live their truth, and refuse to repent.

But Jesus wants to invite you to a better life, a glorious life, to eternal life. He preached: **"For whoever wants to save their life will lose it, but whoever loses their life for me and for the gospel will save it. What good is it for someone to gain the whole world, yet forfeit their soul?"** (Mark 8:35,36).

Don't take the devil's bribe and follow your heart by living in sin. Repent, turn to the Jesus who died for you, and gain something better than the whole world—your soul saved.

NOVEMBER

The Lord has done it this very day;
let us rejoice today and be glad.

PSALM 118:24

November 1

Commander of the Lord's army
Daron Lindemann

What battle are you fighting right now? Jesus leads an army that fights for you.

"Now when Joshua was near Jericho, he looked up and saw a man standing in front of him with a drawn sword in his hand. Joshua went up to him and asked, 'Are you for us or for our enemies?' 'Neither,' he replied, 'but as commander of the army of the Lord I have now come.' Then Joshua fell facedown to the ground in reverence, and asked him, 'What message does my Lord have for his servant?' The commander of the Lord's army replied, 'Take off your sandals, for the place where you are standing is holy.' And Joshua did so" (Joshua 5:13-15).

Notice the striking similarities between this call to Joshua and the encounter when **"God called to [Moses] from within the bush"** (Exodus 3:4). Moses was commanded to take off his sandals because it was holy ground. Divine territory.

The commander of the army of the Lord was the Lord Jesus himself before he physically came to earth at his birth, now appearing to Joshua.

The commander was obviously divine, because he laid out military orders for conquering Jericho that would never work by even the most sophisticated earthly forces. But they did work! Divine victory!

What battle are you fighting right now? Jesus leads an army that fights for you. Listen to him, your Savior and Commander. His promises and commands connect you to the divine!

November 2

God's care for the hurting
Andrea Delwiche

In the Old Testament, God had a clear track record of caring about the poor and helpless. He commanded his people to do the same. God's history of standing up for others is rock solid in the writings of the prophets and the witness of the Psalms. Psalm 140 says it well: **"I know that the Lord secures justice for the poor and upholds the cause of the needy"** (verse 12).

The heart for hurting humans that God demonstrated in the Old Testament showed itself in Jesus. In the gospel of John, Jesus says, **"Anyone who has seen me has seen the Father. . . . Believe me when I say that I am in the Father and the Father is in me; or at least believe on the evidence of the works themselves"** (14:9,11). What Jesus said and did demonstrated what remains important to all three persons of the Trinity: Father, Son, and Holy Spirit.

In the gospels, we see that Jesus enjoyed spending time with all sorts of people: socially acceptable people, people who lived on the margins, and those who were considered literally untouchable. He ate with everyone. He healed everyone. He taught about the kingdom to everyone. He suffered for and saved everyone, regardless of social or political status.

"The Lord secures justice for the poor and upholds the cause of the needy." How do you interact personally with these words? What reassurances do you gain for your own struggles? Where do you need to adjust in order to follow after your Lord?

November 3

One body, many gifts
Karen Spiegelberg

In 1962 President John F. Kennedy visited NASA. During a tour, he met a janitor who was carrying a broom down the hallway. The president asked the janitor what he did for NASA, and the janitor famously replied, "I'm helping put a man on the moon."

While not a religious example in nature, this paints a beautiful picture of how one member functions within the body of Christ. That janitor faithfully used his skills and talents to the benefit of others and the organization as a whole.

Paul plainly explains this concept in Romans 12:4,5: **"For just as each of us has one body with many members, and these members do not all have the same function, so in Christ we, though many, form one body, and each member belongs to all the others."**

Our wise God gifts each of us in unique ways, and all of us faithfully using our gifts form the body of Christ. And just like our physical bodies, the body of Christ cannot function properly unless all its members are working. That means *every* person is important!

Be encouraged today that the work you do within the body of Christ matters! Maybe you feel unseen or underappreciated in that work, but God sees it and is glorified through it! Thank God today for the ways he has gifted you and those around you!

November 4

The danger of deception
Jon Enter

Do you know of David's deception against King Saul and Ahimelech (see 1 Samuel 19-22)? David was anointed the future king of Israel. King Saul was murderously jealous. Rather than trusting God's providence to avoid Saul's sadistic attacks, David relied on deception. He placed a David-sized doll in his bed and slipped out a window when soldiers came to arrest him. He convinced Jonathan (Saul's son) to lie about David's location. David fled to Nob and lied to the priest, Ahimelech, when he asked why David was unarmed. Ahimelech gave David a sword. Then David hid in the enemy Philistines territory and pretended to be insane so King Achish would let him go. Lies. On top of lies. Wrapped in lies.

When you lie, other people get hurt. King Saul murdered the priest at Nob and 84 other priests for helping David. What lies have you told that have hurt others?

When you lie, you do strange things. David acted insane, having saliva run down his beard and doing other awful things before Achish. What have you done to keep a lie secret?

David knew God chose him as the next king. He had every reason to trust God's protection and not his own deception. You are loved by the Almighty! You are chosen to be his own! You have every reason to trust his protection and love. **"The Lord will rescue his servants; no one who takes refuge in him will be condemned"** (Psalm 34:22). Lies lead to destruction; trusting God brings lasting peace.

November 5

God > money
Mike Novotny

There are times when you'll have to choose between God and money. A job offers you bonus pay for picking up the Sunday shift. A promotion would boost your salary but cost you the time you use for the Word and prayer. A scholarship could be yours if you join the weekend tournament team.

Those moments are tempting because money promises happiness, comfort, respect, and security.

But God promises much more! Buying a new phone or upgrading your kitchen is exciting . . . for a bit. Soon it becomes your new normal. But God is eternally exciting, getting better the more you grasp his love for you in Jesus. Too much money will mess with you, like rich people who become arrogant or lottery winners who end up in ruin, but you can never have too much God. More God means more joy, contentment, and wisdom. Mess up with money, and there will be long-term consequences like bad credit or bankruptcy. But mess up with God, and his mercy will call you back in repentance and meet you with the grace of Jesus.

After warning about the love of money, the apostle Paul wrote, **"Fight the good fight of the faith. Take hold of the eternal life to which you were called"** (1 Timothy 6:12). Avoiding the pull of money is a fight. But there is something better to take hold of—a never-ending life with God through the sacrifice of Jesus.

When the time comes, remember which is the better treasure—God is greater than money!

November 6

Named
Nate Wordell

I remember getting a new action figure and marking "NW" on the bottom of his boot. It was a warning to other eight-year-olds: "This one's mine!"

God did that. When the Israelites were a newborn nation, God put his name on them: **"The Lord said to Moses, 'Tell Aaron and his sons, "This is how you are to bless the Israelites. Say to them: 'The Lord bless you and keep you; the Lord make his face shine on you and be gracious to you; the Lord turn his face toward you and give you peace.'" So they will put my name on the Israelites, and I will bless them.'"** (Numbers 6:22-27).

Lots of worship services end with that same ancient blessing. God is putting his name on you.

These days, I've put my name on something more precious than toys. My children are Wordells whether they like it or not. When they behave, it reflects well on me. When they don't, it doesn't. But no matter how well or poorly my kids behave, for better or for worse, they're mine.

Jesus is called Christ, and you are called Christian. How you act affects how others think of Jesus. God marked you with the sign of the cross at your baptism. He retraces his name onto you whenever you hear his ancient blessing. There is no mischief you could make that can erase what God has written. On your best days and on your worst, God sees you and claims you: "This one's mine!"

November 7

Church needs different people
Daron Lindemann

What would make your church better? Gourmet pastries. Not talking about money so much. Childcare during worship and Bible study. Free car washes on Sundays. The list could go on.

The Bible gives another answer about what would make your church better. Different people. As in replacing you? No. As in changing you. Making you different. Better.

"I urge you, brothers and sisters, in view of God's mercy, to offer your bodies as a living sacrifice, holy and pleasing to God—this is your true and proper worship. Do not conform to the pattern of this world, but be transformed by the renewing of your mind" (Romans 12:1,2).

Make up your mind to be different than this world's culture. That makes a better church. It means giving up what your sinful self likes. That's why the Bible calls you a "living sacrifice." You're not burned to a crisp like an Old Testament animal. You remain living. But you still die.

God's mercy kills your self-centered desire to choose your own way. Instead, you choose God's way. God's mercy puts to death every day your tendency to think, act, and decide like everyone else on social media. Instead, you please God online.

A better church is not as much about offering valet parking on Sundays as it is about your life being an offering to God on Sundays and every day. You are being transformed! That's the best worship, which will encourage and evangelize people at your church.

November 8

Angels in the waiting room
Jason Nelson

My open-heart surgery began at 6:30 A.M. and concluded at 10:30 P.M. That's 16 hours. My wife, Nancy, was in the waiting room the entire time. It was during COVID, so no one was allowed in there with her. My daughter, a nurse in the same hospital, eventually snuck in, but Nancy spent the majority of that long day alone. The doctor never came out to see her or give her updates because he didn't know she was there. And eventually they turned out the lights.

When you are critically ill, people pray for you because they know God **"will put his angels in charge of you to protect you in all your ways"** (Psalm 91:11 GW). But angels don't hover only in the operating room guiding the hands of surgeons. They also hang out in the waiting room holding the hands of our loved ones. Let's pray just as earnestly for them. They need their angels too.

The waiting room can be a bleak desert for the family of a patient. It is an unfamiliar place, and there is no visibility into how things are going under the glaring lights in the OR. They are alone with their thoughts. Alone with their worst fears. And they are probably hungry because there wasn't time to pack a lunch. It hurts me to know what Nancy went through. But I am grateful she was sustained like Israel was in the wilderness with the bread of angels (Psalm 78:25).

November 9

What stands out to you?
Andrea Delwiche

There are only seven verses to Psalm 142. Some parts of David's prayer, written for the situation in *his* life, stand out personally for my own time and place. The words shine, and my spirit takes these living words of God and forms a prayer inside David's prayer:

"I cry aloud to the Lord; I lift up my voice to the Lord for mercy. I pour out before him my complaint; before him I tell my trouble. When my spirit grows faint within me, it is you who watch over my way. . . . I cry to you, Lord; I say, 'You are my refuge, my portion in the land of the living.' Listen to my cry, for I am in desperate need. . . . Set me free from my prison, that I may praise your name" (1-3,5-7).

If you read the psalm for yourself, different verses may stand out to you, magnified like a drop of rain on a green leaf. This personal application is a gift of the living Word of God. Why do our spirits latch on to verses of Scripture? The Spirit calls out to our own spirit, reassuring us, teaching us, upholding us. We can ask the Holy Spirit to make the words alive to us. Ask the Spirit to quench your thirst for God's goodness and to let God's love greet you and give you what you need each day.

What longings does the Holy Spirit fan to life in you as you read under God's tender guidance?

Cast *all* your cares on God!
Karen Spiegelberg

We don't have to look far—probably no farther than the walls of our own homes—to see the effects of worrying and anxious thoughts in our world today. People of all ages struggle in this way. Our gracious God has some helpful words for us in this matter:

"Cast all your anxiety on him because he cares for you" (1 Peter 5:7).

"Do not be anxious about anything, but in every situation, by prayer and petition, with thanksgiving, present your requests to God. And the peace of God, which transcends all understanding, will guard your hearts and your minds in Christ Jesus" (Philippians 4:6,7).

These passages don't tell us to lean on God when things start to get really challenging. No—these passages urge us to go to God with absolutely *everything*, whether big or small. We are to trade in our anxious thoughts for prayer. Paul urges us to place our full dependence on God while thanking him for all he's done for us. As a result, we are given peace that goes beyond our circumstances and guards our fragile hearts.

Take everything to God today, and be comforted that your troubles are never outside the control of your Sovereign God.

November 11

The purity test
Jason Nelson

One of the most insidious pursuits in human history is the quest for purity. Since the first failure of people to be perfect, purity in anything is unattainable. Relentless pursuit of purity by misguided people has led to atrocities, schisms, holding grudges, and deceiving ourselves. The same Bible that urges us to be pure in thought, word, and deed also recognizes that we are destined always to fall short. So then, how shall we live?

The answer is a big hard swallow of humble pie for all of us. Any time we think we passed the purity test, we must face the reality that we were born into and are part of the humanhood of the impure. So we cradle the Lamb without blemish or spot close to our hearts. He went to a cross for us and was sheared of his very life. He was **"punished by God, stricken by him, and afflicted"** (Isaiah 53:4). That was pure injustice for Jesus and pure mercy for us. Impure people like you and me are given his righteousness.

Jesus sanctifies the *pure in spirit.* That is something we can pursue because his Spirit lives in us. We can be grateful constantly and gracious constantly. Those are the hallmarks of a pure spirit. We are grateful for faith and life and every good thing that can be traced to both. We are gracious toward every person we meet because Jesus bore their sins and makes intercession for them as well.

November 12

Give me your last meal
Daron Lindemann

Some friends of mine got together to help a widow. We performed long overdue repairs on her home. She just walked around crying, hugging, and thanking everyone.

What if we had shown up at this widow's house and instead of contributing, we just consumed? What if we raided the fridge and made a feast for ourselves? How cruel!

Would you believe that God did something like that to a poor widow? God sent his prophet Elijah to a famine-stricken, drought-threatened land. Elijah asked a widow for some bread and water. Sadly, she had only enough to make a last little meal for her and her son. Then they would die.

Elijah replied, **"But first make a small loaf of bread for me from what you have and bring it to me, and then make something for yourself and your son"** (1 Kings 17:13).

"First." God wants to be first. No matter who you are. No matter how much you have or do not have. That's not cruel. That's God calling you, calling this widow, to faith in true riches. Elijah continued with some life-changing news that the widow's flour and oil for bread would not run out!

God wants to be first in your life—to be feared, loved, and trusted more than all others. Why? Because God put you first, ahead of his own Son who suffered for your sins in your place. Also, when God is first in your life, everything else falls into place.

November 13

The secret to a stable life
Nate Wordell

What's the secret to a stable life? Jesus told a story about that.

"Everyone who hears these words of mine and puts them into practice is like a wise man who built his house on the rock. The rain came down, the streams rose, and the winds blew and beat against that house; yet it did not fall, because it had its foundation on the rock. But everyone who hears these words of mine and does not put them into practice is like a foolish man who built his house on sand. The rain came down, the streams rose, and the winds blew and beat against that house, and it fell with a great crash" (Matthew 7:24-27).

What's the secret to stability? It wasn't in the builder. The two builders were both doing the best they could with the resources they had. It wasn't in the method. Each builder built as best as he knew how. The difference wasn't in the storm. The same wind and rain hit both houses.

The difference was the foundation. The foundation for a stormproof life is the rock-solid Word of Jesus. He says that you are an imperfect person with imperfect habits and a perfect Savior.

As you work on yourself, don't do it from a position of weakness, as if you are your only hope. Put in the work with both feet planted on the Rock. As you develop healthy habits, don't stress that your life depends on those. Build those habits on a solid foundation, the untouchable love of Jesus.

November 14

Perfectionism
Mike Novotny

How do so many of us end up constantly busy? How does an unsustainable pace become the normal we live with? One of the biggest reasons is perfectionism. When we feel like it has to be or we have to be perfect. We "need" to study more, review the Google doc again, make this the best Christmas party ever. We "can't" settle for a B+ in life much less an average C, so we pick up the pace with no finish line in sight.

Do you or does someone you love battle perfectionistic thoughts? Such thinking is common among Christians, since we value doing our best for God and striving to be perfect as Jesus is perfect (Luke 2:51,52). But the devil twists our eagerness for excellence into a life that doesn't imitate the rhythms of Jesus, who himself **"often withdrew to lonely places and prayed"** (Luke 5:16).

The Bible's ultimate answer to perfectionistic busyness is grace. The undeserved love of Jesus has already made you perfect in the eyes of the One who matters most. On your spiritual report card, Jesus has written a 4.0. On your performance before the Judge of heaven and earth, Jesus has scored you a perfect 10. Your heart is hungry for a job perfectly done, and that job was done for you by Jesus. He has made you perfect in the eyes of God.

You trying to be perfect is a treadmill that never stops. Jesus making you perfect is grace that lets you slow down, sit down, and rest.

November 15

People-pleasing
Mike Novotny

How do so many of us end up constantly busy? How does an unsustainable pace become the normal we live with? Your answer might be people-pleasing.

The church needs volunteers, your sister asks you to babysit, the boss wants you to work overtime, your friend texts about using your truck, your grandkids beg for your homemade cookies, and . . .

It's hard to say no. "No" stings. "No" feels like sin, like selfishness, like something our selfless Jesus would never say. Thus, believing we have to say yes, we (over)commit. Again.

King Solomon urged us to avoid such extreme thinking and balance our lives: **"There is a time for everything, and a season for every activity under the heavens"** (Ecclesiastes 3:1). Overcommitting to one thing (like helping people) means there's no time for "everything" (like rest, recovery, and pondering God's Word).

So how do you break free from the shriek of people-pleasing that fills your head? The gospel. The good news of a God who is pleased with you, who approves of you, who smiles when he sees you. Your heart aches for approval, and you already have it through Jesus. If you need to make everyone happy, you will never stop working and will never actually get unanimous approval (just ask Jesus), but if you have Jesus, you have the approval that matters, the kind that comes from God.

Rest in the gospel today. It will allow you to serve others and then sit down, which is greatly pleasing to our Father in heaven.

November 16

I have to be!
Mike Novotny

There are a few people I love who are so busy that I fear for their future. The insane hours, the constant stress, and the lack of rest add up to my deep concern for an impending heart attack or mental breakdown.

Why are they so busy? They're convinced they have to be. If they don't do the work, no one will. If they don't volunteer for the event, the event won't happen. If they don't step up, the whole thing will come crashing down.

Do you ever feel the same way? Your family tells you to slow down, to step back, but you can't, because if you don't, then what? Who will keep that ministry going? How will that organization make it? So you suck it up, power through, and find a way to make it work.

Tired friend, can I remind you today of the sovereignty of God? *Sovereignty* means that God is in control of all things, including the thing you fear will fail. God knows the best time to start a ministry and end it. God has the wisdom to launch a new idea and to close the chapter. You don't need to save anything. God is good at that job.

"And God placed all things under his feet and appointed him to be head over everything for the church" (Ephesians 1:22). That thing you can barely carry is one of the "things" under Jesus' feet. Let him save it if he wants to. It's time for you to rest.

November 17

An odd confession of faith
Jason Nelson

Folks who aren't sold on God say things like, "If he exists, why would he let bad things happen?" That's an odd confession of faith. Their uncertainty about God's existence is rooted in their firm belief that a God worth his salt would always be good, do good, and want good for his people. They nailed it. Their objections also betray disappointment that their lives haven't gone the way the God they don't believe in must want them to. Therein lies our opportunity. "My life hasn't always gone the way God would want either. You tell me your story, and I'll tell you mine."

Listen to their stories. And I mean listen. Avoid the urge to spout some banal clichés or Christian happy talk that doesn't acknowledge their painful experiences. Politely ask them to explain how those are the fault of a God who doesn't exist. Be genuinely sorry for what they have gone through. And actually, affirm their uncertainty by saying, "Sometimes I'm unsure myself."

Then tell your story. Just the relevant parts. Put some flesh in it, but don't be the hero of your own story. Show them how the God they are unsure about is very sure about them. **"This is what the Lord says . . . 'Do not fear, for I have redeemed you; I have summoned you by name; you are mine'"** (Isaiah 43:1). Lift their eyes toward heaven, because the proof of God's existence isn't always in how life goes but what happens after it ends.

November 18

"Because I said so"
Nate Wordell

Why do babysitters say, "Because I said so"? Is every childcare provider on a power trip? I doubt it. Often, "because I said so" is an abbreviation of a longer explanation that sounds something like, "I could explain this to you, but it would be really challenging for you to understand. So I need you to trust that I have your best interest in mind and take my word for it, at least for now." The kids often have no choice but to go along with it, but when little children are at their best, they trustingly reply, "OK."

When the Bible calls you a child of God, it means he created you. It means that he loves you like the best kind of father. But Jesus adds another layer to the analogy: **"Truly I tell you, anyone who will not receive the kingdom of God like a little child will never enter it"** (Mark 10:15).

Like a little child, sometimes you have no choice but to follow where God leads, especially when you can't make sense of what he's doing. But if you want to experience the kingdom of God, the good life where Jesus leads on earth and in heaven, then know that "because God said so" is shorthand for this: "God could explain this, but it would be really challenging to understand. So trust that he has your best interest in mind and take his word for it, at least for now." When God's children are at our best, we trustingly reply, "OK."

November 19

Prayer, not platitudes
Christine Wentzel

In the emotionally charged aftermath of tragic events usually comes a growing backlash toward the responding platitude, "You're in our thoughts and prayers." This was in the comments section of a recent social media story: "I have a priest for prayers and family and friends for their thoughts." *Hmm.*

The offer of prayer is only good if 1) a prayer is given and 2) it's a prayer of a righteous sinner who believes in the work of the only One who made them right with God, Jesus Christ. **"The prayer of a righteous person is powerful and effective"** (James 5:16).

As for thoughts, while some people can draw comfort knowing they are thought of, thoughts do not carry the power of the Holy Spirit to rise before our Lord, who in turn promises to hear and act in his perfect way and time.

Skeptics of this platitude are saying they want action, not mere words; it makes me pause to examine how my prayer life sometimes plays out. How about you?

The apostle Paul says, **"Rejoice always, pray continually, give thanks in all circumstances; for this is God's will for you in Christ Jesus"** (1 Thessalonians 5:16-18). Improving our prayer lives is an ongoing process. To pray continually means making our lives living prayers, to keep a Christ-like posture always. That means praying in all circumstances—joyful times, tragic times, for yourself, for others. And thankfully, Jesus taught us how to pray: **"This, then, is how you should pray: 'Our Father in heaven, hallowed be your name'"** (Matthew 6:9). Amen.

November 20

Earthly suffering vs. heavenly glory
Karen Spiegelberg

A friend of mine endured the unexpected passing of a loved one and a serious medical diagnosis for her child within months of each other. That seemed like enough suffering for a lifetime, and she endured it back-to-back. Do you know anyone who has endured a great deal of suffering? Whether it was loss, illness, financial burdens, or relational hardships? Maybe it's you. Maybe you have endured more suffering than you ever thought you could bear. If that is you or someone you know, hear these words from the apostle Paul, someone who was familiar with suffering: **"I consider that our present sufferings are not worth comparing with the glory that will be revealed in us"** (Romans 8:18).

Paul is not minimizing suffering. In fact, he's acknowledging the enormity of suffering in this world. But even when our heaviest moments in this world are measured against the glory we will experience in heaven, there is no comparison.

Our Father in heaven loves you dearly, and he is walking alongside you in your suffering. As you endure earthly trials, cling to your Savior. Romans 8 goes on to tell us that *nothing* **"will be able to separate us from the love of God that is in Christ Jesus our Lord"** (verse 39)! In other words—He will never leave you! How awesome to consider the day when all sufferings will cease. You will see your Savior face-to-face and be in glory with him forever.

November 21

The gospel of Isaiah
Jason Nelson

If you are a frequent churchgoer, you have heard a pastor say the familiar intro, "Our gospel reading is from . . ." Then he inserts the name of one of the qualified gospel writers: Matthew, Mark, Luke, or John. Thanks be to you, Lord, for their good news to us. But for me, nobody's news is good-er than the Old Testament prophet Isaiah.

Isaiah's calling was to bring hope to discouraged believers. He spoke tenderly to them: **"Comfort, comfort my people, says your God"** (Isaiah 40:1). Your sin has been paid for. The rough road you are on right now will be leveled out for you. You have a Shepherd who will pick you up in his arms and carry you close to his heart like little lambs. He will give you the strength to walk and then run and then soar on wings like eagles.

Isaiah stops just short of calling Jesus by name. **"He . . ."** (see Isaiah 53). He wasn't that good-looking, and his own community despised him. He wasn't just occasionally unhappy; he was a man of sorrows. He was abandoned on the doorstep of a cruel world by his own Father. He bore our sins when he bore his cross. He was punished so we could have peace. He healed us. He rose to see the light of life and makes intercession for us so we will rise to see the light of life.

This reading is from the gospel of Isaiah.

November 22

Living near Golgotha
Christine Wentzel

Outside Jerusalem in Jesus' day was the skull-shaped hill called Golgotha (a.k.a. Calvary). People lived near the place where the life sentences of criminals ended on wooden crosses. In Hebrews 13, the writer describes how the animals used in their Old Testament sacrificial ceremonies were carried out of the city to be burned. They considered Jerusalem "holy," so anything unclean was put out of the city. John the Baptist described Jesus as **"the Lamb of God, who takes away the sin of the world!"** (John 1:29). Jesus was led out of Jerusalem carrying the cross of our sins to die on Golgotha. He was despised and treated like a criminal. Yet he died and rose for the sins of the whole world.

This dying world still seethes with hatred for Christ and his people. Statistics vary widely, but according to one Christian website, 365 million Christians suffer severe persecution. They live near their own version of Golgotha, yet the Spirit grows their numbers every year. The message of salvation for all is very much needed!

We will grow weary as we share the news of Jesus with the world. We will be persecuted and treated like outcasts. But we will not be overcome by it. Instead, we are fired up in the Holy Spirit and with the help of like-minded friends, we continue to share God's Word.

We are fired up by the grace of our Savior who died on Golgotha in our place and rose to glory for our salvation.

November 23

Take captive every thought
Karen Spiegelberg

The National Science Foundation estimates that the average person has between 12,000 and 60,000 thoughts per day. Furthermore, a significant amount of these thoughts are negative and/or repetitive. What if a record was kept of all the thoughts you think in the span of one day? What captures the most space in your brain?

In 2 Corinthians 10:3-5, the apostle Paul encourages us to think about what we think about! **"For though we live in the world, we do not wage war as the world does. The weapons we fight with are not the weapons of the world. On the contrary, they have divine power to demolish strongholds. We demolish arguments and every pretension that sets itself up against the knowledge of God, and we take captive every thought to make it obedient to Christ."**

Paul is describing the spiritual warfare believers experience when trying to resist anything that hinders their walk with God. He urges believers to take every thought captive to make it obedient to Christ. Challenge yourself today to put this into practice. Challenge every thought that comes through your brain against the truth of God's Word. In doing so, God will strengthen your faith, increase your peace, and draw you closer to him.

November 24

Truth does work
Jason Nelson

Philosopher and psychologist William James (1842–1910) is the father of a school of thought known as pragmatism. Without getting into the weeds of his philosophy, it can be summarized by his own saying: "Truth is what works." I confess that, as a practical kind of guy, I am drawn to that way of thinking. For me, good ideas do indeed work. You can see the results. Or as the pragmatists would say, truth has some "cash value" for those who believe in it.

Truth works, and it is supported by its offspring: facts and honesty. Anyone who bends, twists, hides, or mutilates the truth is lying and making common cause with the father of lies, the devil. The power of truth transcends mere personal utility because truth is a godly thing. It was conceived by God and is embodied in him. Remember what Jesus said: **"I am the way and *the truth* and the life. No one comes to the Father except through me"** (John 14:6). When we recognize the truth, we see something from God. When we accept the truth about ourselves, we come face-to-face with God. When we tell the truth, we are speaking for God.

Discovering the truth today takes rigorous intellectual energy. Too many forces want to keep the truth from us because they know the truth would not work in their favor. That's how powerful it is. I encourage you always to want to know the truth because it will set you free.

November 25

The music of your life
Nate Wordell

If each moment of your day-to-day life made a sound, what kind of music would you be playing? Are you living a cacophonous, screaming, garage-band life? Are you playing a gentle melody that's easy but forgettable? Are you composing a beautifully intricate Bach sonata?

Someone asked me that, and it sent me on a wild introspective guilt trip. I've got a nasty sinful nature that sounds ugly.

That night, I scrolled across an online video where a cat was shrieking horrible noises. (Does your life ever sound like a mad cat?) But some musical genius had edited his video over top of the cat's cries. He found all the right notes to harmonize with the screeches, and he modulated the key of his guitar so that the cat's chaos fit in perfectly. He made that kitty sound like a pop star.

Don't you know that Jesus has made your life a duet? He doesn't just drown you out so nobody can hear your song. He fills in the gaps where you fail and harmonizes so that even your wrong notes fit right in. He wants your life lived out loud in him.

"I have been crucified with Christ and I no longer live, but Christ lives in me. The life I now live in the body, I live by faith in the Son of God, who loved me and gave himself for me" (Galatians 2:20).

And unlike a cat video, you can listen for what the Maestro is playing, and you can play along.

November 26

You can enjoy money
Mike Novotny

In the Christian teaching on financial generosity, it is easy to miss some of the surprising details found in God's Word. Here is one of my favorites: **"Command those who are rich in this present world not to be arrogant nor to put their hope in wealth, which is so uncertain, but to put their hope in God, who richly provides us with everything for our enjoyment"** (1 Timothy 6:17). Did you catch that? God provides us with everything for our *enjoyment*.

You can enjoy, according to this Word from God, everything that your Father has provided for you. You can enjoy the fresh air, the warm sun, the hot coffee, the soft mattress, the streaming music, the spacious kitchen, and everything else. Yes, God wants you to be content instead of greedy for more. Yes, God has a passion for generosity, as proven by the very next verse. But don't miss the kindness of God who doesn't guilt you for the gifts you have been given. He has not commanded every Christian to live in a tiny home and eat ramen noodles for the rest of their lives but instead smiles upon us as we enjoy the abundance of blessings that he has poured into our lives.

Christian, be generous with money. And then enjoy every dollar that is left over. You have your Father's full permission to do so.

November 27 | Thanksgiving Day

A key to thanksgiving
Mike Novotny

After the long journey of ACL surgery/recovery/physical therapy, I played my first soccer game in 15 months. And about 30 minutes into the game, I sprinted to the far side of the goal, leapt/threw my surgical leg into the air, and smashed an epic shot into the goal that would have made *SportsCenter*'s top 10 (if *SportsCenter* covered coed, middle-aged soccer leagues in northeastern Wisconsin).

As I watched the shot hit the back of the net, I was overwhelmed with gratitude. My torn ACL was a ripping reminder that most everything in life is temporary, so we must enjoy it when we can. One day, through injury or age, our abilities to walk around the block, run down the field, drive ourselves to the store, and sip coffee with a certain loved one will be taken away.

But we have today. We have this moment of God's grace. We have this opportunity to appreciate the generosity of God. Paul wrote, **"Rejoice always, pray continually, give thanks in all circumstances; for this is God's will for you in Christ Jesus"** (1 Thessalonians 5:16-18).

What are you grateful for today? The ability to move? Loved ones to share a pumpkin pie with? A God who adores you whether you sprint or sit? Take a moment in prayer to look around the room and see a thousand reasons to "give thanks in all circumstances."

November 28

Jesus cooks breakfast
Karen Spiegelberg

Have you ever thought that a sin you committed was too serious to be forgiven by God? Or maybe it's a sin you consistently battle against and wonder if God could really forgive you after falling into that sin yet another time. Perhaps you've seen this struggle in someone else. That person grasps the weight of their sin but does not comprehend the enormity of God's grace and forgiveness.

I wonder if Peter wrestled with that after he denied knowing Jesus three separate times. Maybe he questioned if Jesus could forgive such a bitter denial and wondered if it would affect their relationship.

John 21 records the account of Jesus' third encounter with the disciples following his resurrection. Some of the disciples, including Peter, had been out fishing all night. That morning, Jesus called out to them from the shore to **"come and have breakfast"** (verse 12).

This may not seem like any extraordinary invitation from Jesus, but the implications of it certainly are. Jesus was doing the simple, loving act of cooking breakfast for his disciples, one of whom denied knowing him only a couple weeks ago. If Peter did have any lingering doubts whether Jesus forgave him and loved him, I suspect this beautiful act from his Savior squelched those doubts.

This same Jesus who cooked breakfast for his disciples cares for you too! What a humble God you serve. He forgives you, loves you, and cares for your every need.

November 29

When the time for work is finished
Nate Wordell

There's a beautiful prayer found in old worship books and some new ones. It states the obvious—that neither you nor I have the power to make the Earth rotate into the sun's life-giving rays. Neither do we have enough strength to keep our continent safe when we are in the midnight half of our spin cycle. The orbit of Planet Earth is God's business.

But then it states something less obvious. You and I, on our own, are also powerless to complete our task lists, get to the bottom of our issues, and accomplish what we hope for in the future. Sometimes we think that's all up to us, but without Jesus providing our food, giving us our talents, and looking out for us, we'd get nothing done.

That would be terrifying if the God who holds our tiny planet and miniscule lives in the palm of his hand didn't love us. But here's the best news—The most powerful person in the universe loves you. **"See what great love the Father has lavished on us, that we should be called children of God!"** (1 John 3:1).

So we can pray with confidence:

O God our Father, by your mercy and might, the world turns safely into darkness and returns again to light. We place into your hands our unfinished tasks, our unsolved problems, and our unfulfilled hopes, knowing that only what you bless will prosper. To your great love and protection, we commit each other and all those we love, knowing that you alone are our sure defender. Amen.

November 30

Christmas is history

Mike Novotny

The New Testament begins, **"This is the genealogy of Jesus the Messiah the son of David, the son of Abraham"** (Matthew 1:1). The original Greek of this verse literally says, "The document/record/written statement of the lineage/history/genealogy of Jesus." Other translations say, "This is a record of the ancestors of Jesus" and, "The historical record of Jesus Christ."

That doesn't sound like a Christmas "story," does it? *How the Grinch Stole Christmas!* begins, "Every Who down in Whoville liked Christmas a lot, but the Grinch—who lived just north of Whoville—did not." But the New Testament begins with the word *document*. From the beginning, Matthew wants you to know that he isn't making up some heartwarming story about Jesus.

This was a huge deal to the first Christians. They were eyewitnesses and historians who interviewed eye witnesses and recorded history. They named people like Caesar Augustus and places like Bethlehem and dates and times to corroborate the facts of the nonfiction account they were documenting.

You are no fool to believe that Christmas is for real. You are not gullible or irrational or unintelligent. We don't follow this faith just because we were born in a certain place or raised by a certain kind of people. Christmas isn't based on blind faith but rather on eyewitness documents; touchable, visible archaeological evidence; and so much more.

Nostalgia leads to temporary feelings. History leads to joyful faith. Jesus is the latter. Christmas is for real.

DECEMBER

"He will be a joy and delight to you,
and many will rejoice because of his birth."

LUKE 1:14

December 1

Full of his glory
Linda Buxa

Uzziah became king at age 16—and started off strong. He ruled for 52 years but ended weakly. So when he died in seclusion with leprosy, the people of Judah wondered what the future would hold.

The prophet Isaiah brought some certainty to an uncertain time. In a vision he **"saw the Lord, high and exalted, seated on a throne; and the train of his robe filled the temple"** (Isaiah 6:1). Plus, six-winged angels (seraphim) flew around calling, **"Holy, holy, holy is the Lord Almighty; the whole earth is full of his glory"** (verse 3).

God's glory is easier to imagine when we picture him seated on his throne or when we visit majestic mountain locations or during powerful worship services. But when the seraphim say *the whole earth* is filled with his glory, they mean it. God's glory brings certainty to an uncertain time, whether it's in government or work or churches or relationships. It also means his glory fills the places we consider mundane: where we change diapers, clean out the dishwasher, or fix a flat tire. It fills the operating room and the thrift store where we volunteer and the baseball stadium where we cheer on our kids.

When we're nervous about the present (or the future), when we don't feel noticed, when our hearts are yearning for something this world can't provide, Isaiah's vision is a good reminder: The Lord is still high and exalted and holy. He's the only thing certain in a world of uncertainty.

Because he is holy, holy, holy.

December 2

Can't unsee it
Matt Ewart

There are some things in life you just can't unsee.

For a long time, I struggled to use public drinking fountains because I had seen a small child wrap his entire mouth around the part where the water comes out. It was disgusting. Even though it only happened once, it affected the way I saw every drinking fountain.

The apostle John had a moment like that. After sprinting to the tomb on Easter morning, he stooped to look inside. At first, he hesitated. But when he finally stepped in, he saw the grave clothes with no body in sight. Something clicked.

John didn't understand how it all fit together yet. He didn't even have the biblical understanding to explain what he saw. But when he saw the tomb, here's how he describes himself: **"He saw and believed"** (John 20:8).

With a multitude of questions that had yet to be answered, he had seen something he couldn't unsee, and it shifted his entire worldview.

Maybe faith has been hard for you. Not because you don't want to believe but because of what you've seen. Pain. Injustice. Silence. Hypocrisy. God sees it too. But he also shows you something else. Something that rewires how you see everything: An empty grave. A risen King. A love that didn't walk away.

John saw and believed. He wrote down what he experienced so that you might too. When faith gets tough, imagine if you saw what John saw. It might just change everything.

December 3

Faith like Noah's
Nathan Nass

It had to be hard to be Noah. Can you imagine building a huge boat in the middle of dry land? If you've ever heard the story of Noah and the flood (Genesis 6-9), you wonder how he did it. Other people must have mocked him: "You're a fool, Noah! There's no way it's going to rain that much!" How did he do it?

By faith. Only by faith. The Bible tells us: **"By faith Noah, when warned about things not yet seen, in holy fear built an ark to save his family. By his faith he condemned the world and became heir of the righteousness that is in keeping with faith"** (Hebrews 11:7). It was all by faith.

By faith Noah believed God's words about things he couldn't see. By faith Noah trusted God's promise that God would save his family through the ark. By faith Noah was willing to condemn the whole world rather than turn away from God. By faith God gave Noah the gift of righteousness that comes by faith.

Wouldn't it be great to have a faith like that? May God give all of us a faith like Noah's.

Dear God, in your grace, grant me a faith that builds an ark even before it rains. Grant me a faith that trusts in your Word even when no one else does. Grant me a faith that clothes me in Jesus' righteousness and forgiveness. Grant me a faith that never turns from you. Amen.

December 4

Can drones deliver like Jesus?
Daron Lindemann

Here in Texas, Amazon has begun using a new drone for delivery. The MK30 is designed to carry packages up to about five pounds and operate at speeds over 60 mph. At the delivery address, the drone hovers 10-15 feet above the ground and then lowers the package on a tether until gently releasing it onto a driveway or backyard.

Although Amazon's Prime Air program has received Federal Aviation Administration approval, there's still plenty of skepticism. What about all those wires on telephone poles, not to mention gun-toting Texans taking a shot or three at the drones?

Amazon has offered assurances about these concerns, planning to expand drone delivery soon. Until then, the uncertainty of Amazon drones reminds me of a much more certain delivery of a much more prime package.

"The Word became flesh and made his dwelling among us. We have seen his glory, the glory of the one and only Son, who came from the Father, full of grace and truth" (John 1:14).

Jesus was delivered to us as a gift from heaven. Not just dropped out of the air, maybe to survive, maybe to be blown away, but to live among us.

Keep this Bible verse handy. Bring up the topic of drone delivery in your conversations with friends who don't yet believe in Jesus or need an invitation to church. Ask what they think about Prime Air and what they think about Jesus—the most certain delivery our world has ever received.

December 5

When the siren sounds
Linda Buxa

The small town where my kids went to high school has a fire siren that sounds every evening at 6 P.M. (Don't confuse it with the tornado siren, which is tested the first Wednesday of the month at 11 A.M.) When the siren sounds anytime other than 6 P.M., you know the volunteer fire firefighters are being called into action. They quickly arrive at the station to help their fellow neighbors.

When it comes to loving and helping others, God says we are all first responders. We are called into action when our neighbors need help. Maybe the tragic car accident made the news, perhaps you get a prayer request through church, or you see on social media that someone lost their house to a fire or flood or earthquake. Sometimes the siren isn't quite so public, and you get a desperate text or a tearful phone call or a confession over coffee. As members of the body of Christ, we have all signed up to help quickly when these sirens sound.

"Therefore if you have any encouragement from being united with Christ, if any comfort from his love, if any common sharing in the Spirit, if any tenderness and compassion, then make my joy complete by being like-minded, having the same love, being one in spirit and of one mind. Do nothing out of selfish ambition or vain conceit. Rather, in humility value others above yourselves, not looking to your own interests but each of you to the interests of the others" (Philippians 2:1-4).

December 6

Divine GPS
Christine Wentzel

One day I made lunch plans with a friend in an area completely unfamiliar to me. Soon I was lost and couldn't make out my scribbled notes of directions. Instead of calling my friend, I pridefully determined to figure it out on my own. After a time, I caved in and called her. She immediately came to my rescue, and I followed her to her house. She possessed an amazing grace even though she should have been frustrated with my delay.

As I followed her, I thought, *"Wouldn't it be nice to have a GPS to tell me when I'm taking a wrong turn in life?"* Then it hit me. I do have a GPS—we all do. It's called God's Positioning System. Through the work of the Holy Spirit in our baptism and regular partaking of the Lord's Supper, through prayer and studying God's Word, the Holy Spirit constantly recalculates our positions/choices every time we get offtrack. His calming voice leads us back to the heaven-bound road. We only need to listen and follow.

God's Positioning System is always at work. He responds to our needs and prepares our hearts to learn valuable personal and spiritual lessons.

Here is a shout-out for the amazing grace of the divine GPS at work right now for us all! **"And we know that for those who love God all things work together for good, for those who are called according to his purpose"** (Romans 8:28 ESV).

December 7

Christmas is for nobodies
Mike Novotny

My friend Brad, a pastor at a local Christian high school, once told me what he noticed from walking the halls with hundreds of teenagers. He said, "If you're not smart, athletic, musical, or beautiful, high school can be really hard."

If you're smart enough for high honors, college bound with a bright future, you're somebody. If you're fast enough to make varsity and strong enough for all conference, you're somebody. If you sing at the talent show or can play a guitar around a fire, you're somebody. If you're the cute one they whisper about, you're somebody. But if you're not, you ask, "Who am I? Am I somebody who matters?"

This is why I love the intro to Matthew's gospel, because Matthew notes all the nobodies. **"Ram the father of Amminadab, Amminadab the father of Nahshon, Nahshon the father of Salmon . . ."** (1:2-17). Sure, the list contains some Bible A-listers like Abraham and David, but how many of you could write a Wikipedia page on Ram, Nahshon, or Salmon? I couldn't. Matthew could have stuck to the stars, but instead he gave us this long list of mostly nobodies.

Why would he do that? Maybe to make a point that even nobodies are somebody to God. Even if you're as unknown as Amminadab and Nahshon, God knows you, loves you, cares about you. You don't have to increase your GPA, boost your résumé, or Botox out the signs of your age to get God to smile. Because of Jesus, you are somebody who matters to God!

December 8

The boundary lines have fallen in pleasant places
Dave Scharf

King David was a blessed man. No one before or after him could boast of the breadth or richness of Israel's kingdom, with the possible exception of his son Solomon. But King David was not a blessed man for those reasons, not primarily anyway. David pictured himself looking out from the porch of his palace, and he rightly assessed, **"The boundary lines have fallen for me in pleasant places; surely I have a delightful inheritance"** (Psalm 16:6). David was using a physical picture to describe a spiritual reality. His greatest blessing was in God's promises to send a Savior from sin.

In some way, we can all relate to David's picture by looking at the physical blessings God has poured into our lives. He provides our "daily bread" and often so much more! He gives us family, friends, faith, and the fellowship of believers! Pleasant places, indeed! But it's not just material blessings. Our greatest possession can be seen in our Savior Jesus! The Father in heaven sent a substitute for the life that we could not live and to die the death that we deserved to die. Jesus gave his life on a cross and rose from the dead, assuring us that we too will rise.

God has given us a delightful inheritance in heaven! Because of that, no matter what our physical circumstances, we can say with David, "The boundary lines have fallen for me in pleasant places!"

December 9

Why?
Christine Wentzel

As a kid, I went through a period of intense "why" questioning, hounding my elders on how they knew what they knew. There were two answers that stood out: "I don't know; I just picked it up along the way." Or, "You'll know as you get older." Frustrated, I didn't want to wait for the years to catch me up to them. I wanted to know it all NOW.

As I walk around in my 60+ rotations of the world, I've discovered that instead of finding all the answers to my questions, the more I dig, the more complicated things get. Take for example the human cell. When I was young, it was thought to be a simple composite of water, inorganic ions, and carbon-containing molecules. Now scientists have learned that the more they can see, the more complicated it becomes. Fascinating!

"For you created my inmost being; you knit me together in my mother's womb. I praise you because I am fearfully and wonderfully made; your works are wonderful, I know that full well" (Psalm 139:13,14).

Isn't this a wonderful portion of God's Word to assure us he is at work in all the wonderfully tiny details of creating a person in the womb of a mother!

With this in mind, I can also declare, "I know that full well." And that is more than enough for me to know when I persist with my why questions.

December 10

The reason we're sorry
Dave Scharf

Why are we sorry for our sins? Sometimes, fear drives it. What's the first thing you say to a police officer who pulls you over for speeding? "Oh, I'm sorry, officer!" Are you sorry for speeding or because you got caught?

Listen to King David. He does not say, "Lord, I'm sorry because I fear your punishment." He does not say, "I'm sorry because I got caught." He does not say, "I'm sorry so that you forgive me." Instead, he appeals to God for forgiveness because he already knows God's love—it's what a child of God wants to do.

"Do not remember the sins of my youth and my rebellious ways; *according to your love* **remember me, for you, Lord, are good.** *For the sake of your name,* **Lord, forgive my iniquity, though it is great"** (Psalm 25:7,11).

David knows he is forgiven because he knows God's love. It's why he's sorry for his sin, not because God will hurt him but because he knows it hurts the God who loves him when he sins. David then gives us the key to a repentant life and the focus of our walk in such simple words: **"My eyes are ever on the Lord, for only he will release my feet from the snare"** (Psalm 25:15).

Never take your eyes off Jesus. Remember just how much God loves you, and then you will see the reason to be sorry is because God has forgiven you.

December 11

Faith like Abraham's
Nathan Nass

Do you like moving? How about moving to the other side of the world? How about leaving your parents and other relatives behind? How about doing all that without even knowing where you are going?

In the Bible, Abraham did all that. How? By faith. **"By faith Abraham, when called to go to a place he would later receive as his inheritance, obeyed and went, even though he did not know where he was going"** (Hebrews 11:8). By faith Abraham left his extended family and moved all the way from Ur on the eastern side of the Middle East to the land of Canaan in the far west.

How could he do that? Abraham trusted that God was with him. He trusted that God's plans for him were better than whatever plans he had of his own. He trusted that God was able to provide for him wherever he was. Most of all, he trusted that his true home was in heaven. We're all just strangers here.

Wouldn't it be great to have a faith like that? May God give all of us a faith like Abraham's.

Dear God, in your grace, grant me faith to believe that since you are with me, I am never alone. Grant me faith to let go of my plans and live out the life you have given me. In all of life's moves, grant me faith to trust that my real home is in heaven through faith in Jesus. Amen.

December 12

I want to see it to believe it!
Dave Scharf

Doubting Thomas needed to see that Jesus had risen to believe it. Let's face it. I want to see it to believe it too. "Lord, though you've promised to supply my need, I won't believe it until I have enough padding in the bank account." Sadly, even then, I often don't believe it. "Lord, you tell me everything will work out for my good. I won't believe that until my life is filled with what I call good." I want to see it.

Jesus is here with you today through his Word to say to your doubting and frightened heart: **"Peace be with you! . . . Put your finger here; see my hands. Reach out your hand and put it into my side. Stop doubting and believe"** (John 20:26,27).

Can you see it? Look at Jesus' hands, those nail-scarred hands. They are the hands that spent an entire lifetime doing only good, the hands that carried a cross of wood and all the sins of the world with it, the hands that were pierced for your doubts and fears. These are the same hands that now hold you up in times of trouble and guide you through your darkest days. These hands will one day lift you to heaven, where you will see fully! The hymn writer beautifully wrote: *"He lives to silence all my fears; he lives to wipe away my tears. He lives to calm my troubled heart; he lives all blessings to impart."* Stop doubting and believe!

December 13

Keep your eyes focused
Linda Buxa

My husband and I have a monthly membership to a fabulous car wash. (We need to wash off all the salt needed to keep our roads clear in winter.)

Every time I drive in, I keep my eyes focused on the employee who tells me if I can drive straight in because I'm lined up with the tracks—victory!—or if I should adjust right or left. After that though, I have a hard time keeping my eyes on him as he tells me to drive ahead. That's because there's a car in front of me! I dart my eyes back and forth between him and the car. It seems I don't actually trust him to tell me when to stop.

My life seems a lot like that. God tells me to follow him straight on the path he has for me. I'm okay with that, for the most part-ish. (I mean, we all know I don't follow him perfectly.)

But then when there's trouble in front of me, I dart my eyes back and forth between him and the problems I'm worried about. It's like I don't trust that he knows the plans he has for me, that he will work all things for my good, that he is the refuge I can turn to when I'm afraid.

I could use a subscription reminder to read—and trust—Psalm 141:8,9: **"But my eyes are toward you, O God, my Lord; in you I seek refuge; leave me not defenseless! Keep me from the trap that they have laid for me"** (ESV).

December 14

Christmas is for naughty people
Mike Novotny

Have you ever seriously considered the scandals linked to the first page of the New Testament? **"This is the genealogy of Jesus the Messiah the son of David, the son of Abraham"** (Matthew 1:1). Abraham doubted and then slept with a young woman he wasn't married to. David also slept with a woman he wasn't married to and then had her husband murdered like some B.C. mob boss. And yet here are their names, right next to the name of Jesus.

Apparently, Jesus is not ashamed to be near sinners. Even the ones who lied, covered up their sin, violated their vows. The sexual broken, the money hungry, the exiled. Jesus says that any sinner, every sinner, can turn from their sin and be with him, that his birth in that manger and his death on that cross were sufficient to pay for all of it, every bit of it. Yes, even the worst of it.

So if you are a sinner, Christmas is for you. You might feel unworthy. You and I are unworthy! But Jesus didn't let your unworthiness or my sinfulness stop his goodness. This good news of great joy is for all people; it's for you. This peace is for those who believe. This hope of heaven is for all who call on his name. Let this long list of hard-to-pronounce names in Matthew 1 be the simple proof that Christmas is for you.

December 15

We need a David
Dave Scharf

With whom do you identify when you read the story of David and Goliath? Hopefully, not Goliath! I'm guessing it's David. But you and I are NOT David in this story. We are David's brothers, cowering in the hills as our enemies defy the living God. We are not David, but we want to be.

Too often, we hear that this story is about slaying the giants in our lives. That's appealing because we all want to be like courageous David facing down our giants. But if we read this story that way, thinking we can take down our giants, we will always be disappointed. As one theologian once said, "When we make ourselves the hero of our story, life becomes a tragedy."

You don't need to be more like David. You need a David, and so did he! David said, **"For the battle is the Lord's, and he will give all of you into our hands"** (1 Samuel 17:47). David's greater son, Jesus, went into battle with Satan and crushed his head by his cross and empty tomb.

If someone says to you, "You can fight Goliath!" I want you to ask that person, "How? He's lying there dead with his head cut off!" Jesus has already defeated "Goliath." Far better than your own efforts and works, far better than a few smooth stones, Jesus now gives you the weapon of his Word to silence the devil. As the reformer Martin Luther wrote, "One little word can fell him."

December 16

No excuses
Linda Buxa

God was calling Moses to lead his biological people out of slavery from his adoptive people in Egypt. Moses questioned God's plan though. "Why me? What should I say? What if people don't listen? I'm not eloquent." His final excuse was more of a plea: **"Pardon your servant, Lord. Please send someone else"** (Exodus 4:13).

About 3,500 years later, it's frustrating to see the ways Moses tried to get out of doing what the Lord called him to do. I mean, what was he thinking?! GOD was giving him a job to do, and he was trying to ditch responsibility?

But then I think about my excuses when I see ways I could serve but don't really want to. I'm busy or tired. It's someone else's turn. I don't have the gifts for that. This means I'm probably more like Moses than I care to admit.

Maybe today I should stop overthinking it all. Wherever I am, whomever I meet, I should just serve. After all, God prepared the good works in advance for me to do, so I do them, whether I am gifted at them or not. See, it's not about me; it's about serving the people God put around me and bringing glory to him. No excuses.

There is a caveat though. God does give you rest as a gift. You don't have to do it all, and you shouldn't. But when God calls you, give it your all, all for God's glory.

December 17

Cast yourself to Jesus
Matt Ewart

For many people, hardship isn't the greatest test of faith. Success is.

Just ask Peter. After a long, unsuccessful night of fishing with six other disciples, a voice from the shore told them to cast their nets on the other side of the boat. They did, and the net nearly burst with a miraculous catch of fish.

John turned to Peter and said, **"It is the Lord!"** And immediately Peter went into action. **"He wrapped his outer garment around him . . . and jumped into the water"** (John 21:7). Rather than casting himself into his success or clinging to the catch, Peter instinctively cast himself toward Jesus.

That's not always our first instinct.

When things go well, we might feel compelled to stay in the boat and admire what we've accomplished. We focus on the achievement, admire the full net, and double down on "our work" that got us there. We cast ourselves into our calendars, platforms, and goals, hoping they'll carry us somewhere fulfilling. It's easy to forget the One who saw fit to let us experience success for his purposes.

What will you do today if you find success? You might experience an answered prayer, a productive day, or a win at work or home. Just don't forget who filled the net. Like Peter, let success be a reminder to cast yourself to the One who stands waiting at the shore. Rather than casting yourself into your success, cast yourself to Jesus.

December 18

Am I generous?
Mike Novotny

"**Command them to do good, to be rich in good deeds, and to be generous and willing to share**" (1 Timothy 6:18). Being generous is as commanded in the Bible as being kind, not murdering, and practicing forgiveness. But what exactly does "generous" mean?

The Greek word that Paul uses in this passage is rather unique, only showing up here in the entire New Testament. It is a compound word that combines three ideas. First, *giving*. Generous people open their hands to give instead of clenching their hands to keep. Second, giving *over*. Generous people don't just open their hands for other people to see; they actually hand over what is inside their hands for others to have. Finally, giving over *well*. Generous people hand over wealth well, in a cheerful and willing and repeated way, as opposed to grudgingly, sporadically, or only because they were forced to.

Combining those three ideas gives us a clear picture of generosity. Generous Christians open their hands to give to others, not because they were guilted into giving but because their hearts were moved by their Savior, Provider, and Sustainer. They marvel at the generosity of Jesus, the God who gave his own life, and they respond by giving freely to others. Generosity, therefore, is part of our discipleship, our walk with God as we seek to be more and more like his Son.

Based on that definition, ponder your own attitude toward giving. Ask yourself, with the help of God's Spirit, "Am I generous?"

December 19

Full of the Spirit
Matt Ewart

On the Day of Pentecost, Peter and the other disciples **"were filled with the Holy Spirit and began to speak in other tongues as the Spirit enabled them"** (Acts 2:4). Because of the Spirit's work through them, thousands of people got to hear the gospel that day, and many were saved.

As impressive as that day was, Peter explained that the same Spirit who filled them up fills us up too. He was quick to quote what the prophet Joel wrote: **"In the last days, God says, I will pour out my Spirit on all people"** (Acts 2:17).

"All people" includes sons and daughters, young and old, men and women alike. The "all people" that Joel and Peter spoke of includes you.

But if you're like most people, there are days you don't feel like you're full of the Spirit. In fact, there will probably be days you feel more like a fraud. Can God work through someone like you? Would God even want to *dwell* in someone like you?

When those days come—maybe even today—remember the power and promise of the Holy Spirit. He doesn't come to you because you've earned it. He is poured out generously by Jesus because of who Jesus has made you to be. Let this promise of the Spirit resonate in your heart today: **"The Spirit himself testifies with our spirit that we are God's children"** (Romans 8:16).

December 20

Save me!
Nathan Nass

Save me! Do you ever pray that? Does life get so overwhelming that you don't know what to do, that you don't even know what to pray? All you can say is, "Save me!"

You're not alone. The Bible doesn't hide the depths that believers in God find themselves in. David said: **"Lord, do not rebuke me in your anger or discipline me in your wrath. Have mercy on me, Lord, for I am faint; heal me, Lord, for my bones are in agony. My soul is in deep anguish. How long, Lord, how long? Turn, Lord, and deliver me; save me because of your unfailing love"** (Psalm 6:1-4). Sound familiar?

There's more. How bad did it get? **"I am worn out from my groaning. All night long I flood my bed with weeping and drench my couch with tears. My eyes grow weak with sorrow; they fail because of all my foes"** (Psalm 6:6,7). A flood of tears. Weak from sorrow. What could he pray? Just, "Save me!"

But that didn't mean David was hopeless. Far from it. He trusted in God's unfailing love. He knew this: **"The Lord has heard my cry for mercy; the Lord accepts my prayer"** (Psalm 6:9). He had hope in the Lord.

You do too! God loves you with that same unfailing love. Jesus has saved you from sin and death by dying on a cross and rising from the dead. Take heart! There's hope! The Lord hears your prayers.

December 21

Christmas is about submission
Mike Novotny

Recently I read about the four-year-old son of a lawyer whose teacher told him that recess was over and that it was time to come inside. And this preschooler (the child of a lawyer, remember) turned to the teacher and stated, "I will take that under advisement."

One of the hardest things for humans to do is to submit. When someone insists, "You shall," we think, "You shall not" say that. Whether it's our mom or our manager, the president or our pastor, we don't love being told what we "must" do. Our natures crave independence, and we rebel when anyone attempts to rule over us.

Sooner or later that same struggle happens with God. Jesus never tells you to "be you" or to "follow your heart." No, Jesus calls himself King and Lord, the God who gives the commands and gets the last word. He invites you to repent of your desire to live life your way and, instead, to do life his way.

Why would you ever do it? Why not live your truth and follow your heart? Because this same Jesus saved you. Even before he was born, an angel said, **"You are to give him the name Jesus, because he will save his people from their sins"** (Matthew 1:21). Two thousand years ago, Jesus submitted to the will of his Father in heaven, and the result was your salvation.

What love! What sacrifice! What a compelling reason to trust Jesus and submit everything and every day to his gracious rule!

December 22

Maintaining foundations
Jason Nelson

"**For the foundations of the earth are the Lord's; on them he has set the world**" (1 Samuel 2:8). Please pause for a moment and think about that. What are the foundations of the world?

We know they are the Lord's. They originate with him. They are sublime and ordinary. They include a universe we can't comprehend, the environment we live in and explore, and institutions that give us orderly lives. We need them all and cannot take them for granted.

My list of foundations includes the family, the church, and democratic governance. These institutions are the Lord's, and he has set the world on them. We can trace their durability throughout history and see how they undergird civilization. On them many good things are built. Just pause for a moment and think about that.

I'm thinking about schools, hospitals, law enforcement, the justice system, and picnics by the lake. All the things that give us knowledge, safety, security, and enjoyment are the Lord's. They rest on the foundations of the world. And we must not take them for granted. Please pause for a moment and think about that. And please don't stop thinking about that, because you are the Lord's and he set you in his world. Everything you do has an impact on its foundations.

We might banter about innovations, disruptions, even revolutions. Extremists want to burn it all down. Pause for a moment. We can change the world, but we must be careful to maintain its foundations.

December 23

Confidence comes down
Matt Ewart

"You will receive power when the Holy Spirit comes on you; and you will be my witnesses" (Acts 1:8).

Most of us wait to feel confident before we act. But in God's kingdom, confidence doesn't originate from a feeling within. It's a power that comes down from above. This becomes clear in the first two chapters of the book of Acts.

After Jesus died, the 11 remaining disciples were fearful doubters, hiding behind locked doors. But 50 days later, they were bold proclaimers. Where did this confidence come from? It didn't just come from their internal convictions. Though they had undeniable proof that Jesus was alive, that's not what gave them confidence. And it didn't just come from their calling. Even though the resurrected Jesus commissioned them to go make disciples, that's not what gave them confidence either.

The thing that changed them was power from above.

And when the Holy Spirit came, that's exactly what they received. These unqualified men were empowered to do the unimaginable—speak the wonders of God in languages they had never learned.

The same Spirit who empowered them lives in you. He doesn't wait for you to have the perfect personality, ability level, or track record. The confidence he gives derives its power from above you, not within you.

So don't let hesitation win. Don't wait until you feel ready. The Spirit's power isn't earned by your performance. It's part of being a baptized, forgiven child of God.

December 24 | Christmas Eve

Christmas is about Jesus
Mike Novotny

In his brief telling of the Christmas history, Matthew conveys something essential about Christianity. **"What is conceived in her is from the Holy Spirit. She will give birth to a son, and you are to give him the name Jesus, because he will save his people from their sins"** (Matthew 1:20,21).

The name Jesus, which was a common Jewish name, literally means "The Lord saves." What does Jesus save us from? Our sins. Not our sin, singular, but our sins, plural. The multiple mess-ups, the dumb sins we went back to, the second and third and thousandth strikes against us. Jesus saves us from that.

And the angel didn't say that Jesus would only save people from their not-so-bad sins or their socially acceptable sins. No, it just says, "Their sins," implying that this is an all-inclusive offer from Jesus. For our stubbornness, our anger, our pride, our porn, our homosexuality, our homophobia, our impatience, our unkindness, for yelling just because we were losing an argument or staying quiet when we should have spoken up, for all the wrongs we have done and rights we didn't do, Jesus saves us. The promise is denser and sweeter than dark chocolate—Jesus saves his people from their sins.

This Christmas is likely to be another blur of parties, presents, sweaters, lights, trees, ornaments, food, drink, relatives, and more. In the midst of the madness, I hope you can catch your breath and whisper, "Christmas is about Jesus, the God who saves his people from their sins."

Christmas Day | **December 25**

Christmas kept God's promises
Mike Novotny

The best relationships—the ones where you feel secure, safe, relaxed, really happy—are with people who keep their promises. The worst relationships—the ones where you feel insecure, unsafe, anxious, afraid, really unhappy—are with people who don't. Isn't that true? If your dad promised to show up for your game, your concert, your whatever, and he did, you knew you were loved and learned to trust his word. But if he didn't, you didn't. If your best friend promised to save you a seat, hang out on Saturday, keep your secrets, and she did, I bet you had so much fun as friends. But if she didn't, I bet you didn't. Relationships rely on promises kept.

And that is so true with God. Some people have an amazing relationship with God because they believe he keeps every promise he makes. Despite their sin, they believe God's promise that they are forgiven. Despite their struggles, they believe God has a plan for every day of their lives. Despite not seeing him, they believe that God is with them, for them, behind them, beside them, within them. And they live with this supernatural peace, this ability to breathe and be still.

Child of God, you too can have a faith life like that. Remember that God is not a liar, a deceiver, a trickster, or forgetful. He is truth telling, never exaggerating, always fulfilling. **"God, who does not lie, promised"** (Titus 1:2).

December 26

Sleep in peace
Nathan Nass

Lying awake at night is the worst, isn't it? It usually means there's something wrong. You're anxious about a big decision. You worry that someone might find out about your sin. You can't imagine how you can complete tomorrow's to-do list. So you lie awake.

You don't have to. In the Bible, King David learned to say, **"In peace I will lie down and sleep, for you alone, Lord, make me dwell in safety"** (Psalm 4:8). David learned to sleep in peace.

That's remarkable, considering all the reasons David had to lie awake at night. He spent years of his life fleeing from evil King Saul. He carried the guilt of his sins of adultery and murder. He had many failures as a parent. His own son Absalom rebelled against him. David had lots of reasons to lie awake.

But he had one greater reason to sleep in peace: "For you alone, Lord, make me dwell in safety." The Lord was with him! His guilt was washed away by God's forgiveness. His life was safe in God's hands. His future didn't depend on David. It depended on God's perfect plan. What could David do? Sleep in peace.

So can you! Whatever guilt weighs down your heart, Jesus has forgiven you! Whatever worries you have about your future are really in God's hands. All the to-dos of life don't depend on your strength. They depend on Jesus, and he is always faithful. Tonight, you can sleep in peace!

December 27

This is what God can do
Dave Scharf

Abram wanted a child. Year after year passed, but no child came. Well past childbearing age, Abram cried, **"Sovereign Lord, what can you give me?"** (Genesis 15:2). Can you relate to Abram? Have you asked God, "What can you give me?" Listen to God's answer to Abram's doubts: **"Look up at the sky and count the stars. . . . So shall your offspring be"** (Genesis 15:5).

When tempted to doubt God's promises, step outside and look up at the stars. When tempted to think that he doesn't remember you, remember that the One who promises to provide for you is the One who put the stars in the sky and knows each one by name! He knows you. He will provide. That's what he can give you! This same God put a special star in the sky at Jesus' birth and moved it over Bethlehem. He will make your difficult situation work for your good. That's what he can give you! This same God darkened the sun on Good Friday to prove that your sin really is forgiven. That's what God can give you! This same God made the sun rise on Easter morning to reveal that his Son had risen from the grave! Death is not the end. That's what he can give you!

The next time you're tempted to ask God, "Sovereign Lord, what can you give me?" just look at what he has already done.

December 28

A prayer for wisdom
Nathan Nass

A man recently admitted to me, "I've lost all confidence in making long-term decisions." I bet you can relate. How often does it seem like you make the wrong decision? You and I are faced with dozens of decisions every day, from choosing an entrée at a restaurant to deciding between two schools to weighing different job opportunities. How often does it seem like you always make the wrong decision?

It's humbling, isn't it? We're not as smart as we think we are. We're not as wise as we pretend to be. We have so little control over what the future holds. If we always pick the wrong sandwich, how could we possibly pick the right job?

Young King Solomon recognized this. He recognized the need for godly wisdom. It doesn't come from us. Wisdom comes from God. So one night God appeared to Solomon. He generously said to him, **"Ask for whatever you want me to give you"** (1 Kings 3:5). Wow! What would you have asked for?

Solomon prayed: **"Give your servant a discerning heart to govern your people and to distinguish between right and wrong. For who is able to govern this great people of yours?"** (1 Kings 3:9). What a wise prayer!

Dear Lord, give us discerning hearts. Fill us with godly wisdom to prioritize you and your Word in everything we do. Help us distinguish between right and wrong. Most of all, grant us wisdom to believe in Jesus Christ our Savior. Amen.

December 29

Write yourself a copy
Linda Buxa

The Israelites had been wandering in the desert for 40 years and were about to enter the land God had promised to give them. Because Moses wouldn't be going with them, he gave a list of final guidelines. Included in those were instructions for their future king, which would help the king remain humble, which would bless his life and the lives of the people he was leading.

"When he takes the throne of his kingdom, he is to write for himself on a scroll a copy of this law, taken from that of the Levitical priests. It is to be with him, and he is to read it all the days of his life so that he may learn to revere the Lord his God and follow carefully all the words of this law and these decrees" (Deuteronomy 17:18,19).

This is great advice for us too. Current research shows that taking notes by hand leads to increased comprehension and better recall. So maybe we should consider not just reading God's Word but writing it on note cards or sticky notes or a journal or the back of our hands. As we use our hands to write the words, his hope, joy, peace, comfort, grace, and mercy will sink into our hearts and minds even more.

Then put those notes where you'll see them frequently—a bathroom mirror, your car, your purse, your desk—and read them and follow them. This will bless your life and the lives of the people around you.

December 30

Teach us to number our days
Nathan Nass

The email came as a shock. One of our family's doctors had been gone for one appointment. We didn't think anything of it. He was in his 40s. His office had pictures of him and his smiling wife and children on the walls. Maybe he was on vacation or had that day off.

But then we got the email: He had died. That doctor who always seemed full of life, that doctor who had big dreams for his young family, that doctor got cancer. Treatments didn't work. He died. It was a shock.

We never know, do we? We never know how much time we have left. Sure, we like to think we're invincible. We like to tell ourselves that what happens to so many others won't happen to us. But we never know, do we? All the education . . . All the money . . . All the family support . . . It can't stop death.

That's why 3,500 years ago, Moses prayed to God: **"Teach us to number our days, that we may gain a heart of wisdom"** (Psalm 90:12). Wisdom comes through numbering our days. Wisdom comes through realizing how frail we are. Wisdom comes from depending on God for everything.

Since we never know when our day will come, today is the day to confess our sins. Today is the day to believe in Jesus. Today is the day to love our families. Today is the day to let our lights shine. May God teach us to number our days.

December 31

Better than a second chance
Matt Ewart

You might hear that God is the God of second chances. It sounds encouraging at first, but it's not entirely accurate.

A second chance implies you failed the first time, and now you'd better get it right, *or else*. It suggests that God is watching with crossed arms, waiting to see if you can prove yourself this time. But that's not how God works.

God doesn't deal in second chances. He deals in mercy and grace.

Psalm 103:10 says, **"He does not treat us as our sins deserve or repay us according to our iniquities."** God doesn't tally up our failures to determine how many chances we have left. His mercy and grace reset the score entirely.

Maybe you've failed at something recently. You didn't live up to your own expectations, much less God's. Perhaps you failed as a parent, a spouse, an employee, or a leader. Part of you might wonder if God is finished with you. You might have even begged God at one time or another to give you a second chance. If you have, here's what you need to know: God's plans don't collapse just because you do. In fact, his mercy and grace often shine brightest through brokenness.

Today, don't waste energy wondering if you've blown your second chance. You haven't. In Jesus, God isn't giving you another shot to prove yourself. He's giving you a Savior who already did.

About the Writers

Pastor Mike Novotny pours his Jesus-based joy into his ministry as a pastor at The CORE (Appleton, Wisconsin) and as the lead speaker for Time of Grace, a global media ministry that points people to Jesus through television, radio, print, and digital resources. Unafraid to bring grace and truth to the toughest topics of our time, he has written numerous books, including 3 *Words That Will Change Your Life*, *When Life Hurts*, and *Taboo: Topics Christians Should Be Talking About but Don't*. Mike lives with his wife, Kim, and their two daughters, Brooklyn and Maya; runs long distances; and plays soccer with other middle-aged men whose best days are long behind them. To find more books by Pastor Mike, go to timeofgrace.store.

Dave Burleton is the chief advancement officer at Time of Grace. In his role, his purpose is to make it a truly joyful and faith-enriching experience to be a partner of Time of Grace in the mission to point people to what matters most: Jesus. Dave and his wife, Sarah, have five children (including two sets of twins!) and are actively involved in the children's ministry and music ministries at their church.

Linda Buxa is a freelance communications professional as well as a regular blogger and contributing writer for Time of Grace. Linda is the author of *Dig In! Family Devotions to Feed Your Faith*, *Parenting by Prayer*, *Made for Friendship*, *Visible Faith*, and *How to Fight Anxiety With Joy*. She and her husband, Greg, have lived in Alaska, Washington D.C., and California. After Greg retired from the military, they moved to Wisconsin, where they settled on 11.7 acres. Because their three children insisted on getting older, using their gifts, and pursuing goals, Greg and Linda recently entered the empty-nest stage of life. The sign in her kitchen sums up the past 24 years of marriage: "You call it chaos; we call it family."

Andrea Delwiche lives in Wisconsin with her husband, three kids, dog, cat, and a goldfish pond full of fish. She enjoys reading, knitting, and road-tripping with her family. Although a lifelong believer, she began to come into a deeper understanding of what it means to follow Christ far into adulthood (always a beginner on that journey!). Andrea has facilitated a Christian discussion group for women at her church for many years and recently published a book of poetry—*The Book of Burning Questions*.

Pastor Jon Enter served in West Palm Beach, Florida, for ten years. He is now a campus pastor and instructor at St. Croix Lutheran Academy in St. Paul, Minnesota. Jon also serves as a regular speaker and a contributing writer to Time of Grace. He once led a tour at his college, and the Lord had him meet his future wife, Debbi. They have four daughters: Violet, Lydia, Eden, and Maggie.

Pastor Matt Ewart was born and raised in Oklahoma and has lived in several different places since then, including Nebraska, Utah, Wisconsin, Colorado, and Alaska (for a summer). He has served as a pastor at NorthCross Lutheran Church in Lakeville, Minnesota, since 2014. Before that he served churches located in Commerce City, Colorado, and Tempe, Arizona. Pastor Matt enjoys being outside, listening to podcasts, and tinkering with things in his free time.

Pastor Daron Lindemann loves the journey—exploring God's paths in life with his wife or discovering even more about Jesus and the Bible. He serves as a pastor in

Pflugerville, Texas, with a passion for life-changing faith and for smoking brisket.

Pastor Nathan Nass serves at Christ the King Lutheran Church in Tulsa, Oklahoma. Prior to moving to Oklahoma, he served at churches in Wisconsin, Minnesota, Texas, and Georgia. He and his wife, Emily, have five children. You can find more sermons and devotions on his blog: upsidedownsavior.home.blog.

Jason Nelson had a career as a teacher, counselor, and leader. He has a bachelor's degree in education, did graduate work in theology, and has a master's degree in counseling psychology. After his career ended in disabling back pain, he wrote the book *Miserable Joy: Chronic Pain in My Christian Life*. He has written and spoken extensively on a variety of topics related to the Christian life. Jason has been a contributing writer for Time of Grace since 2010. He has authored many Grace Moments devotions and several books. Jason lives with his wife, Nancy, in Wisconsin.

Pastor Dave Scharf served as a pastor in Greenville, Wisconsin, and now serves as a professor of theology at Martin Luther College in Minnesota. He has presented at numerous leadership, outreach, and missionary conferences across the country. He is a contributing writer and speaker for Time of Grace. Dave and his wife have six children.

Liz Schroeder is a Resilient Recovery coach, which is a ministry that allows her to go into sober living homes and share the love and hope of Jesus with men and women recently out of rehab or prison. It has been a dream of hers to write Grace Moments, a resource she has used for years in homeschooling her five children. After going on a mission trip to Malawi through an organization called Kingdom Workers, she now serves on its U.S. board of directors. She and her husband, John, are privileged to live in Phoenix and call CrossWalk their church home.

Pastor Clark Schultz loves Jesus; his wife, Kristin, and their three boys; the Green Bay Packers; Milwaukee Brewers; Wisconsin Badgers; and—of course—Batman. His ministry stops are all in Wisconsin and include a vicar year in Green Bay, tutoring and recruiting for Christian ministry at a high school in Watertown, teacher/coach at a Christian high school in Lake Mills, and a pastor in Cedar Grove. He currently serves as a pastor in West Bend and is the author of the book *5-Minute Bible Studies: For Teens*. Pastor Clark's favorite quote is, "Find something you love to do and you will never work a day in your life."

Karen Spiegelberg lives in Wisconsin with her husband, Jim. She has three married daughters, six grandchildren, and has been a foster mom to many. Years ago she was encouraged to start a women's ministry but was unsure of the timing. When her brother died suddenly, it hit her hard—that we can't wait until the time seems right for our ministry; the time is now. And so in 2009, with God's direction, A Word for Women was born. Karen finds great comfort in Psalm 31:14,15: "But I trust in you, O Lord. . . . My times are in your hands."

Christine Wentzel, a native of Milwaukee, lives in Norfolk, Virginia, with her husband, James, and their rescue dogs. After two lost decades as a prodigal, Christine gratefully worships and serves at Resurrection Lutheran in Chesapeake, Virginia. In 2009 she served as writer and coadministrator for an online Christian women's ministry, A Word for Women. In 2022 she accepted a position to become the social media director for the WELS military ministry that sees to the spiritual needs of active duty members serving in the armed forces.

Pastor Nate Wordell is a happy son of the King of the universe. He's absolutely smitten with his wife, Rachel, and he's doing his best to raise two little boys. He's a pastor at Wisconsin Lutheran College and was previously at Mount Olive Lutheran Church in Appleton, Wisconsin, and at Martin Luther College in New Ulm, Minnesota.

About Time of Grace

The mission of Time of Grace is to point people to what matters most: Jesus. Using a variety of media (television, radio, podcasts, print publications, and digital), Time of Grace teaches tough topics in an approachable and relatable way, accessible in multiple languages, making the Bible clear and understandable for those who need encouragement in their walks of faith and for those who don't yet know Jesus at all.

To discover more, please visit timeofgrace.org or call 800.661.3311.

Help share God's message of grace!

Every gift you give helps Time of Grace reach people around the world with the good news of Jesus. Your generosity and prayer support take the gospel of grace to others through our ministry outreach and help them experience a satisfied life as they see God all around them.

Give today at timeofgrace.org/give or by calling 800.661.3311.

Thank you!

TIME OF GRACE